Getting Started with Transmedia Storytelling

by Robert Pratten

ISBN: 1456564684

ISBN-13: 978-1456564681

CONTENTS

INDEX OF FIGURES

1   INTRODUCTION

This document is a kind of choose your own adventure. Although it follows a notional workflow from project inception through to completion many of the ideas are complementary so feel free to dive into those sections that interest you most and span out from there. For those that prefer a more structured approach I'd suggest starting here and reading through to the end of the book.

Much of what is written here has been posted by me to various blogs although most notably Culture Hacker[1]. I'm very grateful to all who have taken the time to comment on those posts or email directly to discuss them.

I started writing what I thought would be a book for independent filmmakers but of course the tools and advice given here have a much broader audience so although I often mention indie filmmakers or make references to movies I hope you can see the applicability to your art form.

I had envisaged this to be a much bigger document but times are changing fast so I thought...well.. better to get out what I have while it's still current! I do intend to update from time to time so please join the Community at TransmediaStoryteller.com to stay in the loop. And of course to share your own expertise.

1.1   GOALS

The purpose of this document is to help the reader get started in transmedia storytelling and to do so in a way that is profitable or at least self-sustaining.

1.2   WHAT IS TRANSMEDIA?

"Transmedia storytelling" is telling a story across multiple media and preferably, although it doesn't always happen, with a degree of audience participation, interaction or collaboration.

In transmedia storytelling, engagement with each successive media heightens the audience' understanding, enjoyment and affection for the story. To do this successfully, the embodiment of the story in each media needs to be satisfying in its own right while enjoyment from all the media should be

---

[1] http://workbookproject.com/culturehacker/

greater than the sum of the parts (See Figure 1).

Figure 1 What is Transmedia?

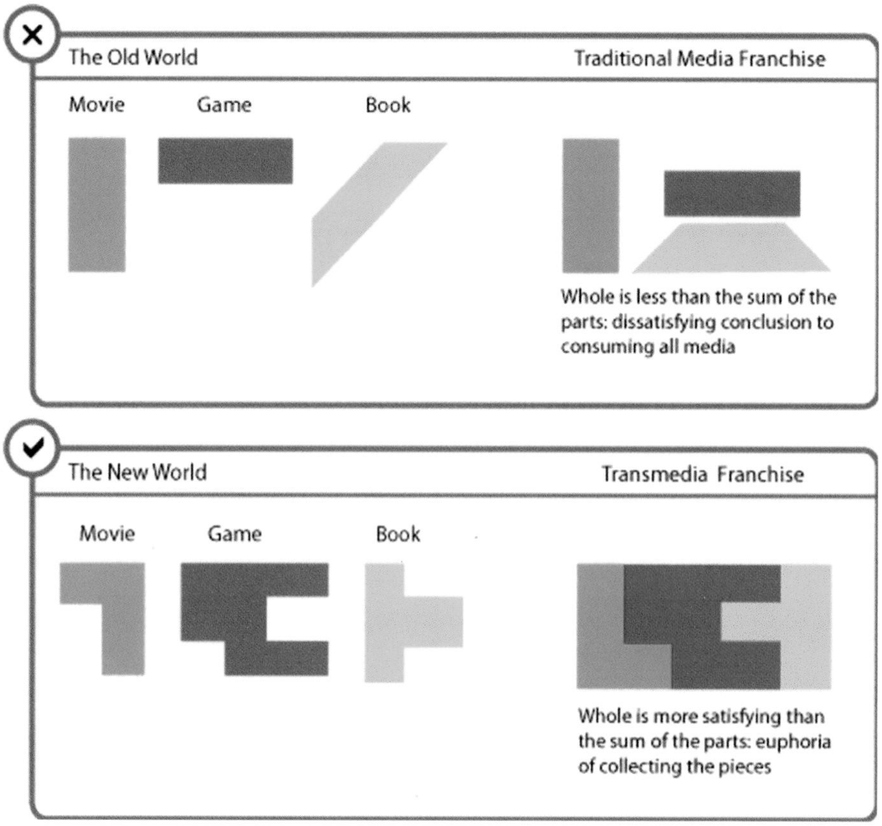

| The Old World | Traditional Media Franchise |
| Movie Game Book | Whole is less than the sum of the parts: dissatisfying conclusion to consuming all media |

| The New World | Transmedia Franchise |
| Movie Game Book | Whole is more satisfying than the sum of the parts: euphoria of collecting the pieces |

This document is about creating transmedia experiences but let's ask ourselves two questions:

- Why would you want to tell stories?

- And why tell stories across multiple media?

1.3   WHY TELL STORIES?

We tell stories to entertain, to persuade and to explain.

Our minds do not like random facts or objects and so they create their own stories to make sense of otherwise discrete, isolated events and items. We naturally and often subconsciously connect the dots. And dots connected in a stimulating way we call great stories.

Great stories win hearts and minds.

1.4   WHY MULTIPLE MEDIA?

We tell stories across multiple media because no single media satisfies our curiosity or our lifestyle.

We are surrounded by an unprecedented ocean of content, products and leisure opportunities. The people to whom we wish to tell our stories have the technology to navigate the ocean and can choose to sail on by or stop and listen.

Technology and free markets have allowed unprecedented levels of customization, personalization and responsiveness such that a policy of "one size fits all" is no longer expected or acceptable.

Telling stories across multiple media – transmedia storytelling – allows content that's right-sized, right-timed and right-placed to form a larger, more profitable, cohesive and rewarding experience.

2 DEVELOPING TRANSMEDIA ENTERTAINMENT

Advising where to start developing transmedia proved more difficult that I thought! In many ways it depends on your starting point, where you want to get to, the context and type of transmedia experience you want to create.

The *Transmedia Project Workflow* presented in Figure 29 is a great overview of a process-orientated approach that works particularly well if you're developing work for clients rather than for yourself. However, it assumes a familiarity with transmedia that you may not yet have.

Documenting and distilling your transmedia project is not a linear process - it's an iterative process. That means you start with some assumptions and cycle through a loop refining, modifying and improving with each pass. The development loop has six key components:

- Story
- Experience
- Audience
- Platforms
- Business model
- Execution.

The goal is to get all six components working in harmony together – supporting and reinforcing each other[2].

Rather than try to tackle all six considerations in a single swoop, allow your ideas to evolve through multiple iterations – start with a small concept, run it through the all the stages and see what comes out. Now start again, this time taking the outputs from each stage and feeding them into the other stages.

In the following sections of the book I'll talk about each stage in detail - so understand that you may not have all the pieces yet on your first pass through. Developing the project in this iterative way makes the process manageable and ensures you think carefully about what you plan to do.

---

[2] When I initially presented my diagram it had only five components as I counted "Experience" as the sum of the others - and it simplified the process. However, I now feel it worth explicit consideration in its own right.

As the project becomes clearer, start to create the documentation and complete sections of your Project Reference Guide[3].

Figure 2 Transmedia Development Process

2.1 THE STORY-EXPERIENCE

Knowing where to start can be the first challenge in creating a transmedia project. The problem is that the story and the *experience of the story* need to be in harmony.

When scriptwriters write a screenplay, how many consider the audience's experience of the movie beyond the emotional engagement with the story? By which I mean, do they think of an audience sat in a cinema; or a couple kissing in the back row of a cinema; or someone with a TV-dinner watching on DVD? The same might be asked of novel writers – do they imagine their readers with book in hand on the beach or sat on an airplane?

I believe the best of all creative people will imagine their audience experiencing their art. That's what enables them to really optimize their creative – the story is in sync or in context with certain audience behavior.

Often the audience experience might be forgotten by some creatives because it's implied or assumed because of the medium: it's a film, it's a book etc. We know what these mediums are.

---

[3] http://www.slideshare.net/ZenFilms/transmedia-project-reference-guide-bible

But a transmedia project can take many forms and guises. Additionally, we want to optimize the advantages that transmedia gives us which is to deliver the right content to the right device and at the right time. That means it's vital we understand the experience we're trying to create: not only the emotional engagement in the story but also in the engagement of the experience.

2.1.1   SO WHERE TO START?

It's difficult to argue concretely what should be considered first, the story or the experience. Writers may choose the story while producers may choose experience.

I come down on the side of sketching out the experience first and here's why.   If you were writing a movie script, you wouldn't write something likely to need explosions, car chases and crowd scenes if it were for a low-budget movie. In that case, you kind of know what "low-budget movie" means. But with transmedia we don't quite know what animal we're writing for without making a few assumptions. That's why we need to consider the type of experience first... and then the story. Although intuitively you may find yourself doing both.

Here's what I think are your core considerations in the story-experience and I'll discuss these in the following sections:

- **The Story**

    – genre, characters, location, time, plot etc.

- **The Experience**

    – timing (considerations: commercial, context, practical)

    – platforms (considerations: media, technology, physical)

    – location (considerations: online, offline, geographical)

    – agency[4] (considerations: interactive, affecting, collaborative)

2.2   THE EXPERIENCE

The varied nature and various forms of transmedia storytelling (see Section 2.3.1) make it particularly difficult to pin down a framework that defines "a transmedia experience". However, I think it can broadly be scoped into four components (see Figure 38):

- **importance of narrative** - how important is the story to the experience? What degree of authorial control is there?

---

4 http://en.wikipedia.org/wiki/Agency_(philosophy) In gaming, how much control the player has.

- **importance of participation** - how important is it that the audience contribute to the story-experience?

- **importance of the real-world** - how important is it that the story-experience pervades real locations, places, events and people?

- **importance of gaming** - how important is it that the audience has a goal or must achieve or collect something?

To further simplify what I think might be the anatomy of a transmedia experience, Figure 3 presents the idea without reference to platforms (e.g. delivery of the experience). Note that:

- all transmedia experiences don't necessarily *need* all three elements to qualify but there probably ought to be a flavor at least of two or more.

- "Gaming" doesn't necessarily mean that there should be "a game" but the mechanics of gaming can be used to stimulate and maintain engagement. Even motivating the audience to jump platforms and the reward for jumping (maybe new content or deeper story) can be helped by simple gaming mechanics. Although I'm not specifically talking about gamification[5], a great online resource to find out more about the sorts of things you might consider is Gamification.org[6].

Participation takes many forms and can run from the "passive participation" of simply consuming content to varying degrees of "active participation" from a Like on Facebook to co-creating content. Figure 4 gives a very nice framework for thinking about types of participation. I discuss participation throughout his document but there's particular reference to it in Section 4.

Figure 3 Anatomy of a Transmedia Experience

---

[5] http://en.wikipedia.org/wiki/Gamification
[6] http://gamification.org/wiki/Game_Mechanics

Figure 4 Forms of Participation[7]

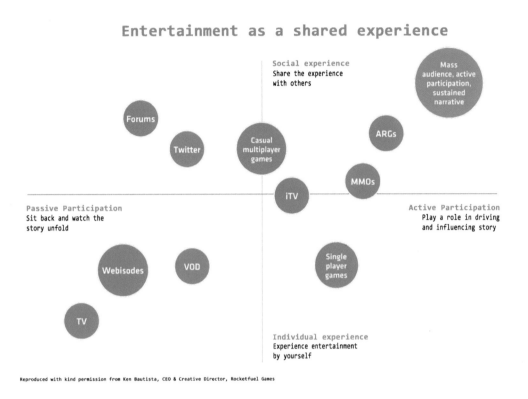

Reproduced with kind permission from Ken Bautista, CEO & Creative Director, Rocketfuel Games

2.2.1 WHAT CREATES A COMPELLING EXPERIENCE?

A compelling experience is one that's engaging - and engagement is discussed in some detail Section 4. But I created this subsection for completeness and to present Figure 5.

The experience design pyramid was brought to my attention by Gene Becker[8] and I think it's a useful diagram because it acknowledges the influence of "sensation".

I believe that sensation is often either overlooked or treated with too much importance to the detriment of the other elements. Glitzy, interactive apps can give that "wow" factor but can hide a lack of transmedia storytelling or a lack of satisfying experience. In these situations, sensation is what Robert McKee[9] might refer to as "spectacle".

---

[7] Reproduced with kind permission from Ken Bautista, CEO & Creative Director, Rocketfuel Games

[8] http://www.slideshare.net/ubik/experience-design-for-mobile-augmented-reality

[9] http://www.screenplayfest.com/ScreenplayFest/PAGES/ARTICLES/Screenwriting/interview_with_robert_mckee_writing.htm

Figure 5 Experience design

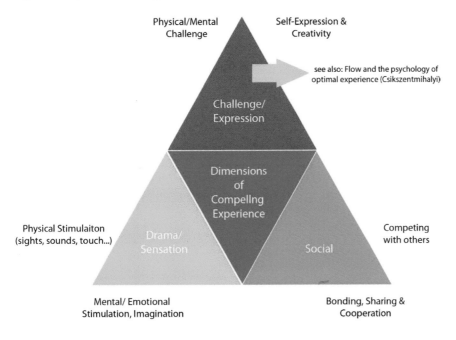

© Hull, Reid "Experience Design for Pervasive Computing"

2.3 THE STORY

Where and how do you start writing your story?

Well, I'd recommend that you start with what you know and branch out from there. But knowing where and how to branch out means considering the type of experience you want to create.

There are five simple questions to ask yourself:

- What is the story I want to tell?
- How will I deliver the story?
- What kind of audience participation do I want or need?
- How will audience participation affect the story over time?
- How much is based in the real world vs a fictional world?

Figure 6 Getting Started: Five Questions

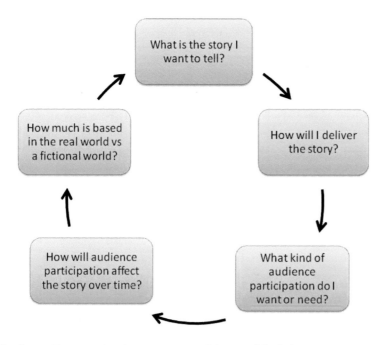

Think of a "story" as one implementation of the world of the story among many potential implementations (see Figure 7). I guess you might think of story as one plot line and associated characters from a world of many plots, subplots, and characters and so on – I've called this a single "narrative space". Figure 8 illustrates how an author might take a single narrative space (one story) and develop it into additional narrative spaces (new stories).

Figure 7 Story vs Storyworld

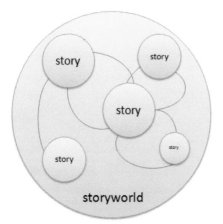

Figure 8 Narrative Space

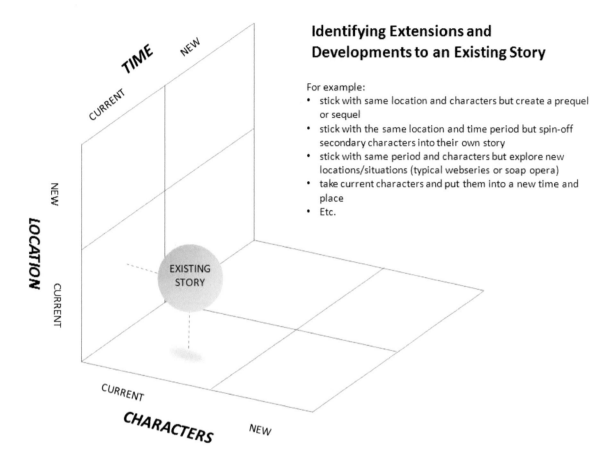

Identifying Extensions and Developments to an Existing Story

For example:
- stick with same location and characters but create a prequel or sequel
- stick with the same location and time period but spin-off secondary characters into their own story
- stick with same period and characters but explore new locations/situations (typical webseries or soap opera)
- take current characters and put them into a new time and place
- Etc.

Ultimately you may have to develop both story and storyworld - and you might have them evolve together - but at this early stage its fine to go where the inspiration and resources take you. You'll certainly need a storyworld document – "a bible" –if you want to attract collaborators or audience participation.

With Parasites (Figure 9) I started with the storyworld because I had a premise that I wanted to explore and a few ideas about a possible plot and nothing else very well developed. With Lowlifes we started with a story and built out the storyworld after we had the first story developed. Note that given the size of the project we never did develop a Bible because I felt it was just overhead for the two of us. Moving forward my thoughts are that I may create a wiki and hoe that the audience might help be document the world.

Figure 9 Initial Idea Creation for Parasites

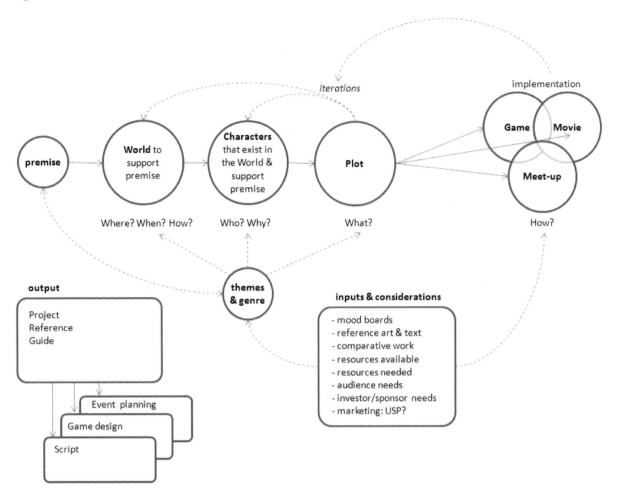

2.3.1 WHAT TYPE OF STORY?

When thinking about delivering the story, put aside the specifics of particular platforms and think about the experience in terms of:

- the narrative spaces you want to cover (location, characters, time – see above)
- the number and relative timing of the platforms (sequential, parallel, simultaneous, non-linear)
- the extent and type of audience involvement (passive, active, interactive, collaborative).

There's a lot to consider here but let's tackle it as a two-stage process:

- Step 1: decide the narrative space, number of platforms and their timing
- Step 2: decide the extent of audience involvement.

2.3.1.1 NARRATIVE SPACE AND RELATIVE TIMING OF PLATFORMS

Figure 10 shows a "typical" Hollywood transmedia project. It's a series of single-platform deliverables - a book, a movie, a game. In many ways the platforms are independent except that they often cover different narrative spaces: prequel, sequel, flashback which may dictate a release order or schedule. In any case there's no apparent audience interactivity between the platforms.

Figure 10 Transmedia Franchise

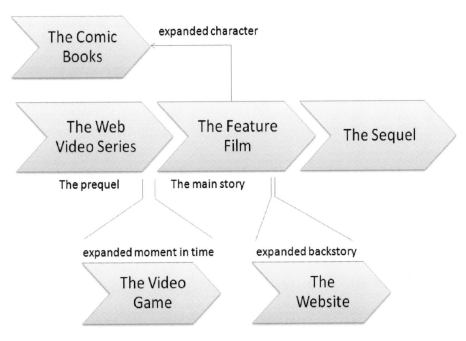

By contrast, an Alternate Reality Game (ARG), Figure 11, might cover a single narrative space across multiple platforms – each alone insufficient to carry the complete story but like jigsaw puzzle pieces they must be assembled to complete the picture (well… you know…   story).

Figure 11 The Alernate Reality Game

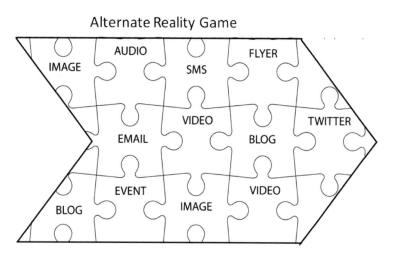

Multiple platforms contribute to single experience

These different types to transmedia can be represented by the diagram in Figure 12.   Of course it's also possible to combine different types of transmedia as shown in Figure 13.

Figure 12 Types of Transmedia

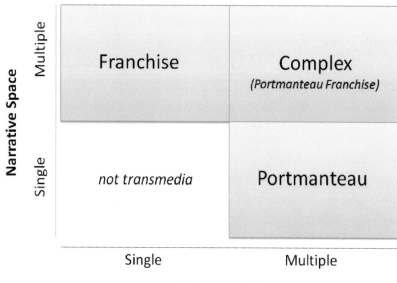

Figure 13 Mixing and Matching different types of transmedia

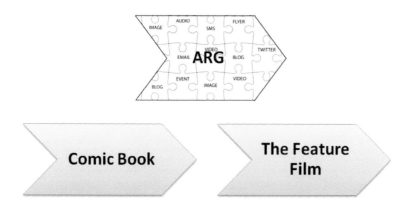

2.3.1.2   AUDIENCE INVOLVEMENT

Audience involvement in the story often bothers indie filmmakers. It's not just that the indie wants to tell his story without interference; it's also the fear that amateur involvement will sully the final result. And for those who have tried involving audiences there's concerns about the effort of "community management" – the time and trouble to guide, motivate, appeal and appease.

It's not only indie filmmakers that worry about how to tell *their* story and yet still find room for audience participation. Talk to game designers about audience (i.e. player) interaction and story and they'll tell you that the more control you give to players (audiences), the less control is retained by the author.   In fact the problem is even more pronounced in MMOs where virtual world guru Richard Bartle[10] says "Virtual world designers can't add story, they can only add content. Content provides experiences that can be made by those who come through or observe them into story." So at its most open-ended, the virtual world (or transmedia experience) creates a world with lots of actionable content and choices but no plot?

This player-author struggle is tackled by games like Fallout3 and Red Dead Redemption (which are console games, not MMOs) by offering players the choice to explore (create their own stories) or tackle quests (follow the author's story). Cut-scenes of course offer the most extreme authorial control.

It's clear that transmedia experiences can borrow from the lessons of games and virtual worlds – creating a storyworld into which the author places a mix of story and content with opportunities for sit-forward and sit-back participation.

Looking further into audience participation I discovered the "storytelling cube" (Figure 14) first presented at the 2002 Game Developers Conference by Raph Koster and Rich Vogel to describe how narrative is explored in online virtual worlds. It applies particularly well to ARGs. The three axes are control, impact

---

[10] http://www.amazon.com/Designing-Virtual-Worlds-Richard-Bartle/dp/0131018167

and context:

- Control: How much freedom does the audience have to create their own experience and how much control will you have as the author?

- Impact: What long-lasting impact will the audience have on the evolution of the experience?

- Context: How much of the experience is based in a fictional world and how much exists in "real life"?

Figure 14 Storytelling Cube (Raph Koster & Rich Vogel)

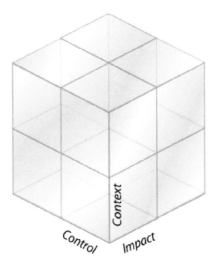

There's no right or wrong position to be inside this cube: it's up to you to decide based on experience, preference and resources.   At one extreme you might have an entirely fictional world, tightly controlled by the author with no audience interaction and at the other you could have an experience based around real-world places & events in which the audience is free to completely change how the story evolves and is experienced. And of course the two can be mixed and there's a lot of space in between.

Having thought through the above considerations, the next three steps will be:

- take a quick pass through the 6-stage development process (Figure 2)

- write down a "high concept" statement

- document your experience

- create your reference material.

2.3.2   WRITING THE STORY

While it's nice to think you might write a story independently of the platform, it's not entirely possible if you want to maximize the audience experience. You only have to take the example of great books that don't translate to movies - the problem is not the underlying story but the failure to adapt it to the platform.

I'd recommend that you start by writing for the platform you feel most comfortable with. Even if your high concept identifies stories on other platforms, complete 99% of one platform and then work on the others. You can then go back to modify or fix the first platform later but trying to write all platforms at the same time will create a monster headache that's worth avoiding!

Note too that it's going to be worth reading up on the specifics of writing for those other platforms because they all have their own rules and best practices.

2.3.2.1   *GOOD STORIES*

There are many reference sources that will tell you what makes for a good story but here are a few bullet points that I believe:

- You need a compelling hero character (protagonist) that people care about

- The character needs to overcome adversity: without adversity there is no conflict and without conflict there is no drama

- Character has a goal – something they must achieve

- Character has needs – typical a primary psychological need that usually fights against the goal (e.g. the need to be liked or the need to save face).

- Character evolves over the story – they start with hang-ups or ill-conceived views of the world and through tackling the adversity they emerge stronger and wiser.

- Good stories have a beginning (setup), middle (conflict) and end (resolution): setup the character and the goal quickly, throw lots of roadblocks at the character that challenge them and that provide learning opportunities (e.g. to deal with their issues) and then wrap up everything –usually hero achieves goal and better understands themselves or changes opinion.

Even if you're writing for a multi-platform/ portmanteau experience such as an ARG, I'd still advocate the need for some form of dramatic structure: there ought to be something that pushes or pulls the experience along. I know there will be those who will violently disagree and there are many experimental and other non-linear narrative approaches to prove me wrong. But if you're an indie filmmaker coming into transmedia for the first time then a dramatic structure will likely serve you best.

2.3.2.2 DEVELOPING THE SOURCE MATERIAL

With the story written for the first platform, you now have source material that can be used to identify additional layers - either smaller exploration content[11] or wholly new complete works (see Figure 15).

In a Franchise approach, I advocate that all the platforms carry equal weight while with the Portmanteau approach the content may well be jigsaw pieces that need to be connected to form a whole experience. Whatever the approach, the narrative should be additive and drive the experience forward.

Figure 16 shows our approach with Lowlifes where we were keen that there should be limited overlap between platforms and that the principal character (the protagonist) of each platform remained the hero of their own media.

Figure 15 Working from source material

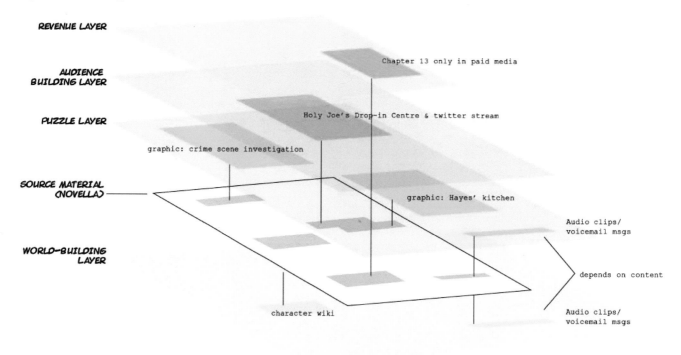

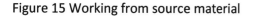

---

[11] See Figure 51

Figure 16 Telling a Story Across Multiple Platforms

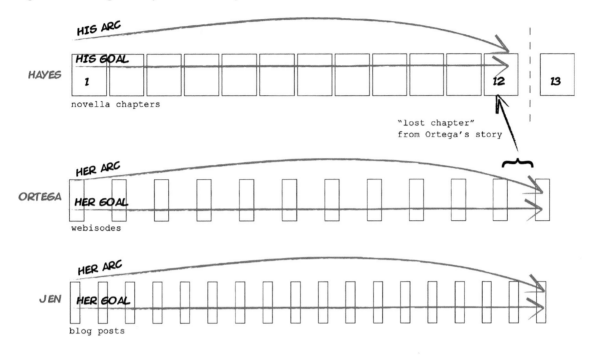

2.4   AUDIENCES – INDENTIFYING AND UNDERSTANDING THEM

For the most part, I'm going to assume that your project is being driven by a creative idea that's dear to you rather than assume you have consumers for whom you need to find a creative idea.

So who's your audience?

There's a good blog post[12] by Dennis Peters that provides a guide for filmmakers on how to find an audience once their movie is complete. But here I'm going to assume you have a transmedia idea and it's not yet started or at least not yet complete.

There are two steps to recognizing your audience:

- identify who they are
- understand what turns them on

In taking these two steps you'll be able to offer the right content, to the right people and the right time.

---

[12]   http://www.heavybagmedia.com/blog/2010/04/06/how-to-find-audience-for-film

2.4.1   IDENTIFYING YOUR AUDIENCE

Below is a list of considerations for scoping your audience. Going through the list below you will be able to identify (and discount) appropriate platforms, when your audience might be viewing or interacting, how big an audience you have and where you might approach them. You should do this:

(a) through the lens of your project's themes, genre and characters
(b) with a particular question in mind (say, regarding business models and likely touchpoints)so as to save you a lot of time and effort.

Note that the objective isn't just to make an exhaustive list of audience characteristics but to prompt you to make better decisions. For any particular decision you may find some data points don't apply. Here's the list:

Socio-economic

- Age & gender

- Income and occupation

- Places where they live (small town/big town/urban/rural) and types of neighborhood (rich/poor/aspiring/hip)

- Price vs time sensitivity

- Brands they like, wear, drive

- Social goals (to fit in/to stand out/to be first/to be life-and-soul/to be kind/to be feared/to be hip/to be traditional)

Media Consumption

- Blogs, magazines, newspapers and books they read; authors they like

- TV shows and movies they watch; directors they like. When, where and how do they watch?

- Music they listen to and bands they like. When, where and how do they listen?

Technology

- Type of cellphone they use (smartphone/basic/old/new)

- Internet speed – at home and at work

- Social networks they use (Facebook, YouTube, Twitter, LinkedIn)

If you're working for a client, you'll likely find they've grouped this data into particular customer segments and given them fancy names such as:

- Gamers

- Students

- Road warriors

- Silver surfers

- Bad Moms with Kids.

You will also have to consider the audience relationship to the client, such as:

- Current Users vs Potential Buyers

- Deciders vs Influencers

- Individuals vs Groups

- Geography (local vs national)

The strength of this segmentation is that it allows us to determine how to better deliver the experience. But it doesn't really provide guidance on what content to provide to entertain them.

2.4.2   ENGAGING YOUR AUDIENCE

When creative people get in the zone they generate a ton of ideas for content and experiences that could all work with their transmedia world. However, with resources always limited, these ideas have to be whittled down to essentials, nice-to-haves and stuff-for-later. One approach is to optimize the mix of content such that it (a) maximizes audience engagement and (b) the longevity (or likelihood of traction) of the experience. In this context I'm using "content" to mean all the things and tools that the audience has at their disposal – from videos, images and text to forums, chat rooms, leaderboards and so on.

If we are to design transmedia projects that engage audiences then we need to understand what it means to be engaged. Most would agree that it's more than just "a view" and that there are probably degrees of engagement ranging from "doing *something*" (like a click) to "*creating* something" (like remixing a video).

2.4.2.1   MEASURING ENGAGEMENT

In 2006, Ross Mayfield stated in his blog:

> "The vast majority of users will not have a high level of engagement with a given group, and most tend to be free riders upon community value.   But patterns have emerged where low threshold participation amounts to collective intelligence and high engagement provides a different form of collaborative intelligence".

He coined the term "The Power Law of Participation[13]" which is shown in his diagram below (Figure 17).

Figure 17 Power Law of Participation

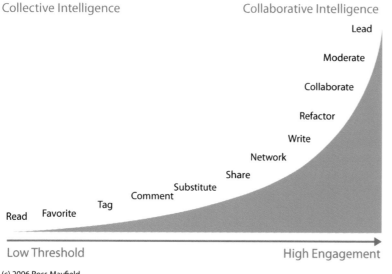

(c) 2006 Ross Mayfield

This participation curve can also be applied to transmedia worlds and will be evident to those who've run an ARG. Figure 18 shows the participation law at work in Mike Dicks[14] diagram "Rules of Engagement".

Figure 18 Audience Participation with Content

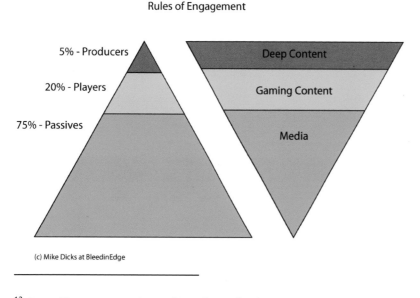

(c) Mike Dicks at BleedinEdge

13 http://ross.typepad.com/blog/2006/04/power_law_of_pa.html
14 http://www.bleedinedge.co.uk/

What this means is that if there's less effort involved in participating in the storyworld (for example watching a video vs remixing a video) then more of the audience are likely to do it but you can't say that they're as engaged with world as those who are expending more effort. More effort on behalf of the audience implies that they must be more engaged, right?   Well, yes and no.

It depends on how the individual audience member derives his or her pleasure from the world. Not everyone wants to or feels able to remix videos or contribute user-generated content yet nevertheless may be a strong advocate for the world – telling friends, family and strangers that they really ought to check out the content. Surely that's an engaged audience too?

Forrester Research identifies four measures for engagement with media content[15]: involvement, interaction, intimacy and influence. Developing this for our purposes of understanding engagement with a transmedia world, we should measure not only the audience's interaction and contribution but also their affection and affinity towards the world – that is, *what they say* and *how they feel* about it.

Taking this approach, a Facebook "Like", while taking such little time and effort, ranks pretty well on the engagement scale. It's more than *just any* click. It's a show of affection.

But to get that "Like" or to get a "Share", you need to provide the mechanism and the content.

Figure 19 shows the three stages of engagement – Discovery, Experience & Exploration – that inform your content choices across my five levels of increasing engagement:

- Attention
- Evaluation
- Affection
- Advocacy
- Contribution.

Figure 19 Measuring Engagement

Stages of Engagement	Discovery		Experience	Exploration	
Level of Engagement	Attention	Evaluation	Affection	Advocacy	Contribution
Content Type	Teaser	Trailer	Target	Participation	Collaboration
Goal for your content	Find me. Fan comes to site and consumes	Try me. Fan increases engagement and consumes	Love me. Fan spends money and decides that	Talk about me. Fan tells friends.	Be me. Fan creates new content

15 http://www.dynamiclogic.com/na/research/whitepapers/docs/Forrester_March2009.pdf

	low-involvement free "teaser content"	free "trailer content"	what I offer delivers on the promise, is entertaining and is worthwhile.		
How	Be relevant	Be credible	Be exceptional	Be spreadable	Be open
Measurement	views, hits, time spent per view, number for content viewed (per channel & content (e.g. emails, blogs, videos, Twitter etc.)	clicks, downloads, trials, registrations	purchases, ratings, reviews, comments, blog posts, Twitter follows, Facebook Likes, joins community	repeat purchases, subscriptions, memberships, Online: reTweets, forwards, embeds, satisfaction polls & questionnaires Offline: focus groups, surveys	Uploads, remixes, stories written, collaborations, number of fan moderators for forum, events held, other UGC

2.4.2.2   *LONGEVITY OF THE EXPERIENCE: THE AUDIENCE ECOSYSTEM*[16]

The purpose of this subsection is to introduce non-game designers to some gaming ideas and concepts that I think can be very helpful in designing participatory experiences - particular when deciding how much and of what type of content to create. The secret to prolonged engagement I feel is to design a self-sustaining ecosystem in which the audience is allowed (given the tools and permissions) to evolve its own experience by generating new content or assuming the roles originally assumed by the designers.

To design a self-sustaining world requires that we understand the audience ecosystem of different types of people motivated in different ways. The world needs a mix of these people to make the experience work.

In his excellent book *Designing Virtual Worlds*, Richard Bartle describes his analysis of MUD player types in which he asked the question "what do people want from a multi-user dungeon?" He concluded that there

---

[16]   When I originally published this section on my blog, Brooke Thompson (http://www.giantmice.com/) who leads the International Game Developers Association (IGDA) Special Interest Group on ARGs quite rightly pulled me up on a few points where I'd misspoken and not thought carefully enough about the point I was trying to convey. I've made the corrections in this document.   She also pointed me to her White Paper which expands on the audience/player segmentation I present here. Brooke's whitepaper can be downloaded here: http://archives.igda.org/arg/resources/IGDA-AlternateRealityGames-Whitepaper-2006.pdf   You can also read online as a wiki here: http://wiki.igda.org/index.php/Alternate_Reality_Games_SIG/Whitepaper

were four player types:

- *Achievers* – like doing this that achieve defined goals such as leveling up, gaining points etc
- *Socializers* – like hanging out with other people (either as themselves or role-playing a character)
- *Explorers* – like discovering new parts of the world
- *Killers* (also known as *Griefers*) – like to dominate and upset others!

Bartle found that each type needed another type in order to sustain their fun and engagement. If you buy his book – which I recommend you do – then you can see how these groups inter-relate to each other.

Bartle also created what he calls a Player Interest Graph – as shown in Figure 20

Figure 20 Player Interest Graph (by Richard Bartle)

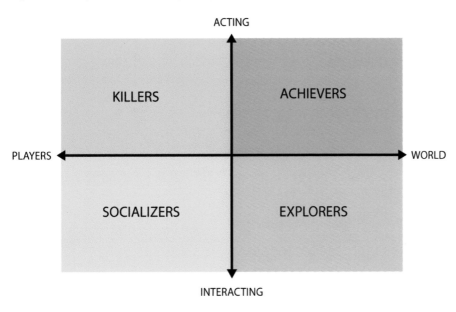

Richard Bartle, *Designing Virtual Worlds*

I was reminded of this diagram recently when I discovered Jane McGonigal's paper on the Engagement Economy[17]. In her paper you'll find a reference to Nick Yee's document on *Motivations of Play Online Games*[18] which has similar findings to Bartle's work.

Also in McGonigal's paper is a reference to Nicole Lazzaro's *Emotional Goals of Players*[19]. In Lazzaro's paper she identifies four keys to unlocking emotion in games (illustrated in Figure 21):

- *Hard Fun* - players who like the opportunities for challenge, strategy, and problem solving. Their

[17] http://www.iftf.org/node/2306
[18] http://www.nickyee.com/pubs/Yee%20-%20Motivations%20(in%20press).pdf
[19] http://xeodesign.com/whyweplaygames.html

comments focus on the game's challenge and strategic thinking and problem solving.

- *Easy Fun* - players who enjoy intrigue and curiosity. Players become immersed in games when it absorbs their complete attention, or when it takes them on an exciting adventure.
- *Serious Fun* - players who get enjoyment from their internal experiences in reaction to the visceral, behavior, cognitive, and social properties.
- *People Fun* - players who enjoy using games as mechanisms for social experiences and enjoy the social experiences of competition, teamwork, as well as opportunity for social bonding and personal recognition that comes from playing with others.

Figure 21 Four Keys to Unlock Emotion in Games

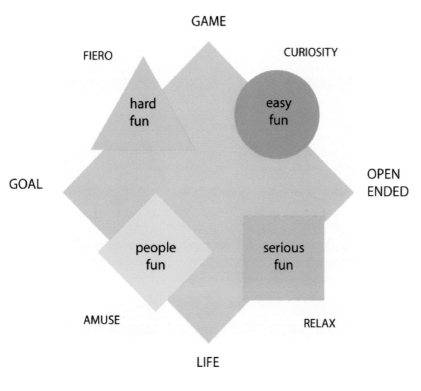

(c) Nicole Lazzaro, www.xeodesign.com

Again, it's possible to see echoes of similar findings to Bartle's work and I decided to map Yee's and Lazzaro's work to Bartle's Player Interest Graph as shown in Figure 22.

Figure 22 Goals by Audience Interest

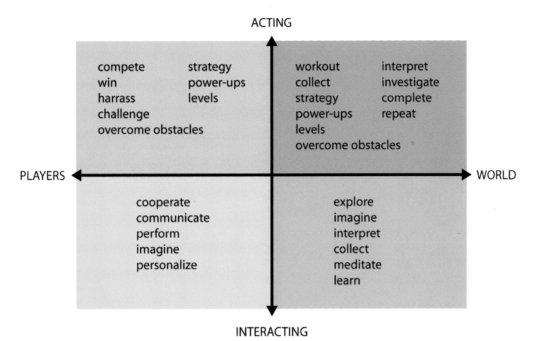

If these are the benefits being sought by audiences, then it's now possible to convert this into a content map that shows what content is most likely to appeal to particular groups of the audience. This is shown in Figure 23.

The importance of this is that we can now check our content to see if we're pulling too hard in one direction; for example, too much content aimed at *Explorers* and not enough content for *Achievers* or *Socializers*.

Always remember that I think of transmedia content as being recursive – meaning that although the ARG is shown here as fundamentally a game, in designing the ARG you would take a more granular approach and look at the specific content of the ARG and how it appeals to each player type.

To summarize then, in designing your content strategy, look to provide something for each of the four audience types and do so in a way that offers opportunity for attention, evaluation, affection, advocacy and contribution.

Figure 23 Content by Audience Type

2.5 PLATFORMS

By "platforms" I mean the combination of media plus technology. So YouTube and iTunes would be two different platforms even if they can both deliver video. A printed book and The Kindle would be two different platforms. A cinema, a living room and an outdoor public space are all different platforms.

Almost any technology, medium and place can be used to convey your story but think about your audience again – what's their lifestyle? Where and how do they hang out? If you've got a story appealing to single-parent families is it likely they're going to attend live events? Maybe if it's during the day and they can bring their babies but most likely not in the evenings – they have problems with babysisters, cash and free time. Which platforms will appeal to this audience?

Think of your project as a lifestyle choice: it needs to slip into your audience' lives with the minimum amount of friction.

Now iterate back to the story. What might you do with the story to have it play out better across these platforms?

2.5.1 PLATFORM SELECTION

As I said above, by "platforms" I mean the combination of media plus technology. In this section I'd like to get you thinking about how you might go about selecting the *right* platforms. Of course there is no universal truth in platform selection – the *right* platforms are those that best suit you and the project.

Although I would advocate that all projects have a community platform but that might not be part of your storytelling.

While keeping in mind the larger iterative development process, I recommend a similar five-stage iterative approach to selecting your platforms:

- Stage 1: go with your gut
- Stage 2: consider the relative strengths and weaknesses of each platform
- Stage 3: support the weaknesses of a platform with the strengths of others
- Stage 4: consider the timing of platforms relative to each other
- Stage 5: consider changes to the story to bake-in the platforms and timing.

2.5.1.1   GO WITH YOUR GUT

In the first instance, just go with your gut and list a few platforms that you think will suit your story and audience. This first pass will likely identify platforms based on the following:

- personal desire or bias
- experience
- popularity with audiences (including fashions and fads)
- ability to collect payment
- availability to find funding or sponsorship
- popularity with the press & bloggers (at certain times some platforms are more sexy that others)
- suitability to the story
- resources available.

Now take a closer look at each platform.

2.5.1.2   DETERMINE EACH PLATFORM'S STRENGTHS AND WEAKNESSES

In determining a platforms' strengths and weaknesses:

- first - consider the experience you'd like to create and which platforms are best suited

- second - rank the short list of platforms and ensure they create a mix that works synergistically

Choosing the right platform for the right experience

A senior executive at Yahoo spoke on Fora.tv recently about how Apple asked Yahoo to design an app for the iPad that would be a "coffee table experience". The idea was that the iPad would be out on the coffee table in the living room when friends visited and the owner would want to pick up the device and share the Yahoo entertainment with her guests. Yahoo tailored its online content to suit the specifics of the iPad – not just the unique form factor but the unique consumption context too.

Device manufactures spend a lot of time thinking about how their products will be used. Learn a lesson from these guys and don't just partition your story across platforms but take time to adapt it so it works in the context of the device and the audience lifestyle.

Table 1 and Table 2 present possible ways to segment your platforms by the nature of audience participation. Use this type of approach to inform the platform selection around the type of experience you'd like to create.

Table 1 Possible platform segmentation 1

	Personal	**Shared**
"Passive" **(Lean back)**	Watching movie: mobile phone, laptop, slate Reading: book, mobile, laptop, slate, Kindle	Cinema TV Theatre?
"Interactive" **(Lean forward)**	Handheld game Mobile Laptop Slate Kindle (interactive fiction)	Multiplayer game Theatre? iPad/Slate? – see comment above

Table 2 Possible platform segmentation 2

Location agnostic		Location-dependent	
Personal	*Shared*	*Personal*	*Shared*
Web series Comic/Graphic novel Motion comic Book eBook Pin (badge)			Poster Event Façade projection mapping[20]
Merchandise		Exhibition	
Mobile game ARG (alternative reality game) AR (augmented reality) Postcards and flyers			

Find the right mix of platforms

Given that each platform will have its own strengths and weaknesses, the goal of this stage is to be objective about why a certain platform should remain in the mix. My recommended approach is to score each platform based on the following criteria:

---

[20] http://www.youtube.com/watch?v=BGXcfvWhdDQ

- Revenue gained
- Cost (inc. time) of delivering content
- Ability of platform to enable social spread of content
- Fit to audience lifestyle
- Remarkability (uniqueness/coolness/timeliness/quality) of platform or content
- Timing of release to audience

The table below shows how these might be scored from 5 to 1 and Figure 24 presents an example from the Excel spreadsheet tool that's available for download at this book's website.

While the exercise feels a little academic, if you have to justify external funding and justify to yourself that it's worth putting time into something, it's worth quickly running through the numbers – you might find some surprising results.

Table 3 Rating a Platform

	Rating
Revenue	Good=5, Poor=1
Cost	Low=5, High=1
Spreadability	Good=5, Poor=1
Lifestyle Fit	Good=5, Poor=1
Remarkability	Remarkable=5, Unremarkable=1

Figure 24 Platform Tool Example

Index	Vehicle2	Platform2	Revenue	Cost	Spreadability	Lifestyle F	Remarkability	Score	Weighting	Final Score
1	Novella	Kindle	5	1	0	3	2	11	2	22
2		PDF	0	1	5	1	1	8	1	8
3		Book	5	3	1	5	2	16	2	32
4		Text	0	1	5	1	1	8	1	8
5	Webseries	YouTube	0	1	5	5	2	13	1	13
6		iTunes	0	2	5	4	2	13	1	13
7		DVD	5	3	1	4	2	15	2	30
8								0	1	0
9								0	1	0
10								0	1	0
11								0	1	0
12								0	1	0
13								0	1	0

2.5.1.3 HAVE PLATFORMS SUPPORT EACH OTHER WITH CALLS-TO-ACTION

Now you know the pros and cons of each platform, you need to find ways to have them support each other. What I mean by this is that some platforms will be great for spreading awareness but lousy at making money. To combine the strengths of each platform means getting the audience to cross between platforms.

So how do we do this? Firstly it's important to remember that crossing platforms introduces friction. So rather than assume that audiences want multi-platform experiences, it's better to ask yourself three questions:

- What's my **objective** in having audiences cross platforms?
- How can I **motivate** audiences to cross platforms?
- What's the **reward** when they get there?

The Call to Action

Before I continue, I'd like to introduce a little jargon: the "call to action".

In web design, the button and wording on a page that asks you to "click here" or "sign up" is known as the "call to action" (CTA). It's a plea for the user to do something and good designers make these calls-to-action appear to be the default choice – you're nudged to take action through clear layout, positioning of the button, use of colors and so on.

The term is also used in advertising: "for a limited time only", "while stocks last", "a once in a lifetime offer". These are all calls to action to get you to do something *now* and not put off your decision.

A transmedia experience needs similar CTAs to get audiences to cross platforms.

What's the objective?

Part of your objective will be to create a fun experience but it will also relate to your business model. Here are three illustrations.

Example 1. A transmedia project has a comic book and a web series: the comic book will carry advertisements because it's believed that print advertising is less intrusive than pre-roll video advertising (because the ads won't get in the way of the story). The value of the advertising is such that it pays for both the comic book and the web series. Both will be given away for free but the advertiser has been promised a minimum number of comic book readers. Hence, it's important to get web series viewers to cross platforms to the comic book.

Example 2. A transmedia project has a mix of free and revenue-generating platforms: the free platforms build the audience and the revenue-generating platforms pay for the project. Your first thought might be that CTAs are needed to ensure the free audience migrates to a revenue platform. But this only provides part of the solution. Table 4 compares the relative audience sizes and revenue potentials across platforms and offers possible strategies to maximize the opportunities. Note that CTAs are used not only to grow revenue but to grow the audience - migrating them to more social platforms and providing spreadable content with CTAs to promote further growth.

Example 3. In my Lowlifes[21] project, physical and device-specific copies of the content is paid content while web-based content is free. My primary, albeit weak, CTAs are:

---

[21] http://lowlifes.tv

- the project "logo" that displays three media types – informing audiences that this story spans multiple platforms
- the story in each media begs questions that the audience desires to be answered – and expects to find them in the other media; hence enticing them to cross platform.

With Example 3 in regard to moving from a free platform to a paid platform, I'm hoping that the friction of being tied to a desktop (free platform) will encourage supporters to migrate to a paid platform for a better experience more in tune with their lifestyle – for example, the ability to read a paperback book in the bath!

In these examples you can see that the business model creates different objectives for cross-platform traversal.

Table 4 Assessing your call-to-action: comparing audiences across platforms

		Audience Size and Loyalty/Enthusiasm		
		Casual Audience		Hardcore Audience
		Big	Small	
Platform Revenue	Biggest Revenue	Big Win. Keep the audience here and keep them spending! Refresh content, allow audience to create content (includes discussions, suggestions, live chat).	Provide CTA's to motivate audience to become Hardcore	Respect this audience: don't milk them for money. Use their enthusiasm to grow casual audience. Invest in community and provide spreadable content with CTAs to build wider audience.
	Smaller Revenues	Small Win. Can a gentle CTA motivate them towards a bigger revenue platform?	Provide CTA's to motivate audience to become Hardcore – more revenue will likely follow.	Maximize spreadability of content (see above). Provide gentle CTA to nudge onto higher revenue platforms.
	No Revenue	If revenue is important, need a CTA to send audience to a revenue platform	How is this platform contributing to the experience?	Maximize spreadability of content. CTAs to grow audience and nudge this audience to revenue platforms.

How do I motivate audiences?

Having decided your objectives, how do you motivate audiences to jump platform?

The one response to this question could well be "if you're having to 'motivate' audiences then surely that's highlighting a weakness in your experience?" I agree with that sentiment but if we'd like the audience to buy something or to be somewhere else for the next part of the experience then some motivation may well be required… just try to be gentle ☺

Digital content can have a nice layout and a URL to prompt action but what about live street theatre performance – how do you get audiences to cross platform from the street to, say, go online? Possible solutions to this example might be:

- flyers with your URL on it (potentially lacks social/real time web)
- flyers with QR code and Twitter #tag
- merch/pins (badges)/bookmarks and other give-away with QR code or #tag
- performers wearing a t-shirt with a QR code or #tag
- the performers verbally encourage the audience to go online (e.g. shout at them!)

These answer the mechanics of "how" and assumes that the live audience has mobile phones (so make sure the online landing page is small-screen friendly). But they don't address "why?"

Motivating the online involvement in this example ought to stress the urgency or immediacy of the situation – don't let the crowd disperse and hope they'll connect later: integrate the online component into the performance. Now you're incentivizing cross-platform activity with the promise of online participation in the live show.

If this isn't possible or appropriate, you need to consider other incentives ranging from blatant bribery with gifts or prizes to simply the promise of satisfying the audience's curiosity about what happens next or explaining what on earth the performance is all about.

Figure 25 illustrates a way to think about what you might need to do to motivate audiences to cross or combine platforms. The diagram shows the audience being acted on by two opposing forces: the incentive to migrate (positive force) and the disincentive to migrate represented by "friction" (negative force). By friction I mean anything that makes crossing platforms a pain: increased cost, additional keystrokes, diverted attention, low bandwidth and so on.

Figure 26 and Figure 27 illustrate the consequences when the opposing forces are of different magnitudes.

Figure 25 Incentive Vs Friction: Motivating the Audience to Cross Platforms

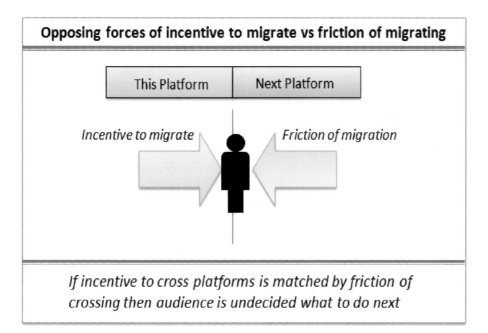

Figure 26 When Incentive > Friction Audience Crosses Platform

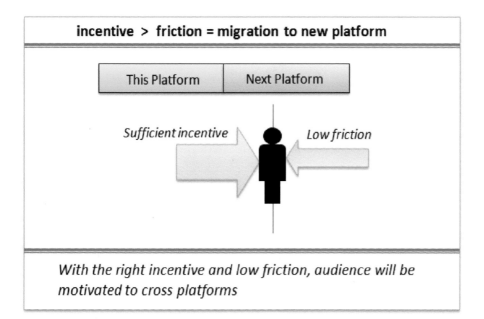

Figure 27 When Incentive < Friction Audience Doesn't Cross Platform

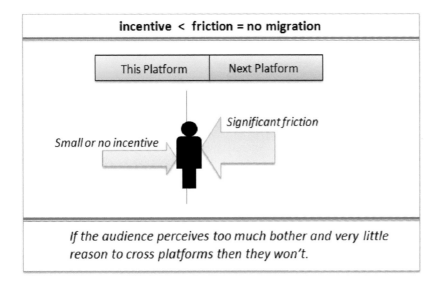

In the example of the street performance, the live activity creates attention and a call-to-action gets them online - but what now? Sell them a DVD? Get them to join a social network or mailing list? It's going to depend on where you are in the project and I'll address this in the next step.

2.5.1.4 PLATFORM TIMING

Unless you have unlimited resources it's likely you'll have to prioritize how platforms are released and to do that it will be helpful to define your objectives. Set your objectives with reference to your business model and resources.

Table 5 and Table 6 provide examples of roll-out strategies dependent on different business models. Note that steps can and may need to be combined or they may overlap. There's no hard and fast rule – the purpose of the approach is get you thinking logically and covering the bases.

Table 5 Example Platform Release Strategy 1

Step	Objective	Platforms
1	Have paid content available to capitalize on interest from day #1	DVD, Kindle, Pay-to-view/download
2	Release free content to build audience	Web series, comic book
3	Attract the hardcore audience	ARG with "secret" comic books and webisodes as level rewards
4	Work with hardcore to spread word to casual audience	Collaborative/co-created sequel

Table 6 Example Platform Release Strategy 2

Step	Objective	Platforms
1	Attract large casual audience	(sponsored & televised) flash mobs
2	Work to convert casuals to hardcore	Social network with unfolding/evolving Twitter story
3	Work with hardcore to spread word to develop experience	User-generated video & poster competitions
4	Sell paid content	DVD, merch, performance workshops/training

Until now very little has been said about the story. It hasn't been ignored – it's been there as a touchstone throughout these five stages – but now is time to see what we might need to do given our platform preferences.

2.5.1.5   CHANGING THE STORY

Think of the story has having two components:

- "the story"   - the whole world that's created with all the characters stretching out in chronological order
- "the experience" – how the storyworld is revealed to the audience (timing and platforms).

Note that the story might be much larger than the project you're working on now.

Our objective throughout this process is to have the story and the experience of the story integrated with the business model.   Although you started with "the story" in mind, platform selection has rightly focused on "the experience". Now is the time to sanity check the experience and see if there's any missing story, story that now needs adapting or story + experience that can be improved.

For example, now you have a roll-out strategy for your platforms (the experience), iterate back through the story and look to improve or create new (in no particular order and please add more):

- Twists
- Surprises
- Cliff hangers
- Inciting incidents
- Reunions
- Breakups
- Conflict

- Discovery
- Exposition
- Reversals
- Suspense
- Threats
- Complications
- Conclusions

2.6 BUSINESS MODEL

The business model explains how are you going to pay for the project. You have three primary choices:

- Sponsored (e.g. free to Audience) - here the project is paid for by the author (self-funded) or by a 3rd party such as a brand (advertising, product placement, branded entertainment) or by benefactors (crowdfunded, arts endowment)

- Audience-pays - purchase of content through paid downloads, physical product, subscriptions or membership

- Freemium - mix of Sponsored and Audience-paid content that may change over time.

Given the importance of financing, I've given it its own section (See Section 5) but here I wanted to look at how you might decide what is the best business model for your project:

- Look at your audience – what do they buy and how do they buy?

- Look at the platforms you're considering – which support the sponsored approach (e.g. social and easily shared) and which support the paid?

Figure 28 illustrates how different platforms lend themselves to different financing methods. I originally created the graphic for a presentation to the Music Business School[22] in London but it's possible to use the same axes and position other platforms more relevant to your project.

---

[22] http://musicbusinessschool.co.uk/

Figure 28 Multi-platform Strategy (Music example)

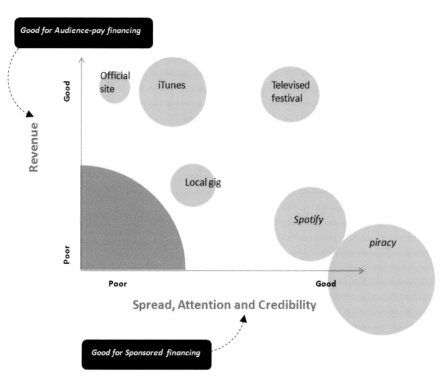

Remember to iterate back to the story and this time think about the experience in terms of the business model. How can you develop your story and platforms to better suit the business model?

2.7 EXECUTION

Figure 29 presents a five-stage workflow for executing your transmedia experience.

The process works like this:

- Define what it is you're trying to achieve. *What's your objective* in creating this experience?

- Develop your ideas further and create a skeleton, a strawman, a framework of the experience. What does this experience look like?

- Design the experience in detail and document how each aspect will be implemented

- Deliver the experience to your audience

- Wrap up the experience once it's run its course.

Figure 29 Transmedia Project Workflow

Definition	Development	Design	Delivery	Wrap
•Goals	•Concept & Synopsis	•Timeline	•Audience building	
•Scope	•Plot & premise	•Languages & geo-restrictions	•Production	
•Success criteria	•Principal characters & cast	•Touchpoints	•Implementation	
•Target audience	•Art direction	•Calls to action	•Testing	
•Business case	•Audience experience timeline	•Scheduled content	•Launch	
•Team	•Design summary (audience/ story/ platforms/ business model/ execution)	•Event-driven content	•Operation	
	•Bespoke technical development	•Interactivity	•Measurement	
	•Business model	•Gaming		
	•Licensing & copyrights	•Asset list		
	•Community management	•Platforms		
		•Capacity planning		
		•Merchandise		
		•Integrated Marketing Communications		
		•Execution		
		•Controls		
		•Mythos		
		•Series synopsis & arcs		
		•Future stories		

The strength of this workflow is that each stage takes the design of the experience to the next level. If you're working for a client who's funding the work, you have natural tollgates at the end of each stage to get sign-off (and payment).

To get started, my advice would be to create a new document from the Project Reference Guide[23] template and start filling in the sections where the inspiration takes you.

I haven't covered all the stages of the workflow in detail in this release of the document simply because I ran out of time! Please sign-up to the Community at TransmediaStoryteller.com or follow me on Twitter to get the updates when they become available.

---

[23] http://www.slideshare.net/ZenFilms/transmedia-project-reference-guide-bible

2.7.1 DEFINITION

The Definition stage has two primary objectives:

- create an executive summary

- put some boundaries on the project.

It's unlikely you can complete this stage without looking ahead at some of the issues in Development and Design but that's not to say that those later stages have to be completed in full before you can finish Definition.

The Definition is a convenient top-sheet that someone more interested in the business side of the project can read without bothering to read how it's implemented. Plus you put some boundaries on the project and document what's going to be possible and what's not.

2.7.1.1   GOALS

If you're creating a project for your own personal satisfaction then your goals might include artistic challenges you set for yourself, financial goals, raising your personal profile, gaining more Twitter followers or maybe some of the possible goals for commercial projects, presented below, might apply too.

If you're creating a project for a client or for a social cause then you'll have one or two (don't try to accomplish more than two because the project will lack focus) of the following business goals which I've grouped into four broad categories:

- Awareness
    - Maintain or boost brand awareness
    - Reach beyond the usual or core consumer
    - Assist in profiling and recruiting influential consumers
    - Generate press (old & new media)

- Advocacy
    - Increase consumer advocacy
    - Reward or empower advocates
    - Add buzz to brands and products
    - Generate fans and followers

- Revitalization
    - Add glitz to boring or undifferentiated products
    - Generate word-of-mouth around low involvement products
    - Build brand image
    - Build product awareness
    - Re-position against competitors

- Sales
  - Generate indirect sales through all the above
  - Increase in direct sales by getting the consumer closer to the point of purchase, combined with sales promotion

A key consideration in goal setting is how much control do you want to concede to the audience and how vital is their participation for success? The implications of this are discussed in the story section.

Remember that your goals should be "SMART": **S**pecific, **M**easurable, **A**ttainable, **R**ealistic and **T**imely. That is, be pragmatic and specific about what you can achieve with the resources you have.

2.7.1.2 SCOPE

The scope will include your high concept and a short synopsis but its principal job is to create some boundaries. Look ahead to the Development and Design stage issues and go through the list to see what you need to address here.

For example, you might say the project will only be in English language, location-based games will be limited to San Francisco although online content will be available internationally and no new technology will be developed.

The idea is that you communicate the ambitions of the project, and address the implications of crewing and budgeting, without yet having to design the whole experience in detail.

2.7.1.3 SUCCESS CRITERIA

In Goals you set yourself some targets; here you explain how you'll recognize when those goals have been achieved.

Note that for goals related to things like awareness and sales, there could be a number of factors that make measuring these problematic such as a lag or continued effect after the project has wrapped or the impact of other events outside your control such as economic collapse, a disappointing product (if it's a new product launch) and so on. Hence try to specific about what tools and metrics you'll use.

2.7.2 TARGET AUDIENCE

Please see the discussion of audience in Section 2.4

2.7.3 BUSINESS CASE

If you've been hired to create an experience then expect the client to provide this information. In this case it's intended to provide background to the project so that you understand why it's believed the transmedia experience is needed.

If you're developing this project for yourself then I'd suggest working on the Development stage first and then writing a summary here. In this case it'll show the financial headlines:

- a cost breakdown of the project by platform and by cost type (capital costs and operating costs)

- a revenue breakdown of the project by source (sponsorship, grants, direct finance, pre-sales, sales and so on)

- break-even analysis (the point at which the total net revenue matches the total costs).

2.7.3.1 TEAM

This is basically your heads of department. If you're working for a client, it may also include members of their staff – for example, those working in community management or public relations etc.

The team might include:

- Executive Producer - financials and overall project success (could be client)

- Transmedia Producer and/or Experience Designer - responsible for developing the transmedia story-experience and execution

- Head Writer and/or Creative Director - responsible for the artistic success

- For each platform

  - Platform Producer

  - Writer

  - Creative Director

  - Various crew depending on the platform ranging from camera crew & costume designers through to software developers, runners, comic book artist and so on

- Marketing Manager/Producer

- Community Manager

- Outside agencies: digital/interactive, PR, seeding

2.8   DETERMINING YOUR RELEASE SCHEDULE

The release schedule describes how often you publish content to your audience. The goal is to profitably maintain engagement between published content. A good illustration of my approach can be given by looking at the webseries as a platform.

Core to my approach is understanding how you want the audience to engage with your story and then designing an integrated experience that consequently determines how each platform - in this case the web video - will be released.

***

Why do some web producers release their webisodes weekly when they have evergreen content? That is, if their series of web videos are not tied to current events, why not release them all at once?

One answer might be that the release schedule is tied to the production schedule - episodes are being produced one week and released the next. But why not release them two weeks apart or wait until enough episodes have been produced to release all at once or daily? Why not four hours apart or on demand?

My point is only that there should be some reasoning behind the scheduling and not just because TV has scheduled weekly content.

You see, if TV has taught us one thing about audiences, it's that they don't like to be kept waiting. They don't like to wait while the commercial plays, they don't like to wait while the episode downloads and they don't like to wait week-to-week. Many people record several episodes of a series before the viewing or they'll buy the complete series on DVD. But of course audiences come to TV and the web with different expectations so why copy the TV model online if you don't have to?

2.8.1.1   RE-THINKING YOUR WEB SERIES

This blog post looks at how you might optimize the release schedule for your webisodes. Core to my approach is understanding how you want the audience to engage with your story and then designing an integrated experience that consequently determines how the video will be released. There is no initial assumption that the schedule should be weekly or any other time period.

There is, I suppose, an assumption that most web series will have more than just the videos: there's usually a website, a blog, a forum, a mailing list, a Facebook page or some other mechanism that represents an opportunity to inform the audience of a new release and provide them with a backchannel. These additional non-video platforms are what makes your web series "an experience" rather than a series of videos. Even a single YouTube channel with the comments and likes enabled creates a participatory experience. Whatever the implementation, it is the experience that builds, empowers and engages your audience - it multiplies the draw of the video.

Here's a short list of considerations for determining the time interval between episodes with the key objective being to maintain engagement between episodes (i.e. you want audiences to watch the next episode):

- production limitations & opportunities

- distribution limitations & opportunities

- business model limitations & opportunities

- strength of story episode to episode (the narrative hook)

- length of each episode (longer webisodes might benefit from   longer periods between episodes to avoid overload)

- audience expectations and headroom (giving too much to consume between releases may lead to abandoned subscriptions).

2.8.1.2   *MIND THE GAP: IS THE NARRATIVE STRONG ENOUGH TO BRIDGE THE DELAY?*

Figure 30 illustrates how we'd like audience to move from episode to episode. In this example there's enough interest or engagement to have them come back for more.

Figure 30 Audience follows episode to episode

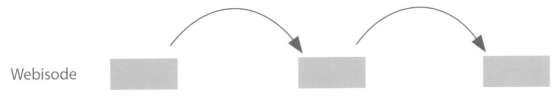

Unfortunately there are a number of failure scenarios if the period between each release is wrong. In Figure 31, the audience abandons the web series because the content isn't strong enough to have them come back - there's not enough pull to bridge the gap.

In Figure 32, the audience is asked to work too hard to keep up and soon they find they're overwhelmed with content for the given schedule.

Figure 31 Abandons

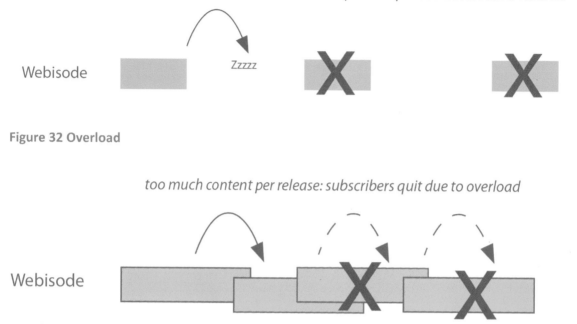

weak narrative or incorrect release schedule causes orphaned episodes that are never watched

Webisode

Zzzzz

Figure 32 Overload

too much content per release: subscribers quit due to overload

Webisode

In both these failure scenarios one solution is to adjusted or fine-tune the schedule - if that's possible. As I mentioned earlier, there may be reasons why you're stuck with the schedule.

Figure 33 Release schedule adjusted

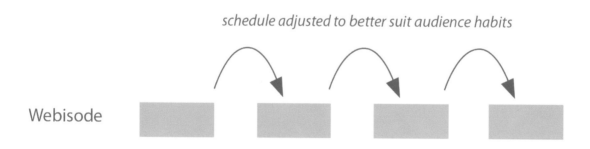

schedule adjusted to better suit audience habits

Webisode

2.8.1.3   USING TRANSMEDIA STORYTELLING TO MAINTAIN ENGAGEMENT

Web series can be expensive to produce and the number of episodes is as likely to be determined by budget as anything else. This could mean you don't have enough webisodes to span the schedule you'd like or you need to maintain engagement between webisodes because the schedule is fixed.

Figure 34 shows how narrative spread to secondary, less expensive, media can be used to stitch together the web series - providing a mid-episode fix of story for those eager for more. The trick here is in the storytelling: to have the webisode and secondary media satisfying in their own right   and hence consuming all media is optional which hence alleviates the chance of overload. Implied in the notion of "secondary media" is that it may indeed not stand alone and should be consumed as additional exploratory content (e.g. another optional layer).

Figure 34 Transmedia Storytelling applied to web video series

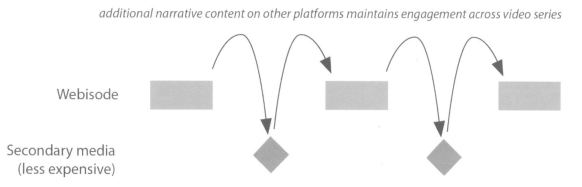

Figure 35 in contrast shows two equal media platforms both scheduled for episodic release but appealing to different audience sub-segments or consumption habits: e.g. media 1 is consumed while at work and media 2 consumed on the commute.

Here, each media has its own (intervening?) release schedule with additional narrative hooks and branches to take the audience to the next episode in the same media or to alternative media.

Figure 35 Native Episodic Transmedia Storytelling

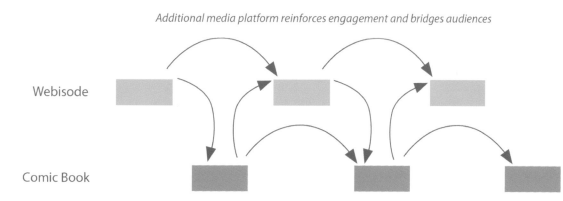

Finally of course, additional secondary media might be added to two primary media platforms - as shown in Figure 36.

Figure 36 Multi-layered Transmedia Story

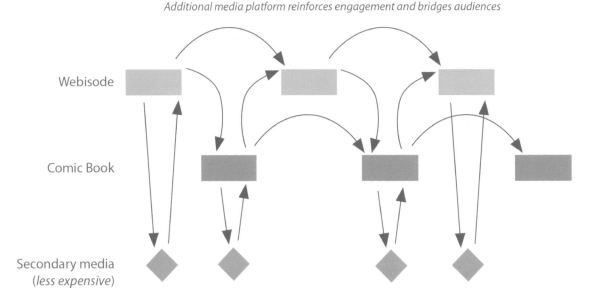

Additional media platform reinforces engagement and bridges audiences

Webisode

Comic Book

Secondary media
(*less expensive*)

2.8.1.4 ALLOW AUDIENCE TO GO WITH THE FLOW

So far I've assumed that all audience members are to be treated equally. But why not reward engaged followers with either additional content or early "pre-release" content? And if you do, does it matter that they might share with others ahead of the "proper" release?

I believe that when you have someone that's engaged you should allow them to ride the engagement out and see where it takes them. This means allowing them to request additional content on demand ahead of the release schedule which I further believe has the potential to turn engaged audiences to advocates - hence recruiting more audience.

YouTube's "Unlisted" video option is perfect for this: casual viewers won't see or find the video before it's made public but engaged audiences can be sent the link.

2.8.1.5 LOWLIFES EXAMPLE

My Lowlifes project has three primary media: novella, webisodes and blog. I determined that it should be scheduled to be released two days apart over a period of 15 days or so. I felt that daily would lead to content overload and at three days the whole release would drag on too long.

One approach would have been to alternate the media - novella chapter on day 1, video on day 2, blog on day 3 and so on. But this would have incorrectly implied a sequence or priority to the media platforms that I was keen to avoid.

Consequently, at the same time content is made public, subscribers receive an email with links to the three media episodes plus the ability to request additional content from anywhere within the series. This would allow someone who was really into the videos, for example, to watch them all in one sitting by simply requesting them.

It's not a problem for me if someone grabs all the videos and posts them all on their own blog because my objective is to get them seen. It's evergreen content and within 3 weeks it would all be available in any case.

For Lowlifes, the scheduling and on-demand requests for content is made possible by a service called Conducttr -a pervasive entertainment platform from my company TransmediaStoryteller.com and will soon be available for all members of our Community.

2.8.1.6   SUMMARY

In summary then, if you assume that the audience always has something better to do with their time and money, it will absolutely focus your mind on maintaining engagement between webisodes and this will:

- determine the optimum release schedule where you have the flexibility to choose it

- highlight the need for a transmedia experience around an inflexible release schedule

- provoke a discussion about whether you should allow content on demand for the most engaged audience members.

3   DOCUMENTATION

My advice is take a pyramid approach to documentation: start with the headlines and allow readers to dive deeper if they wish. In increasing degrees of detail, your documentation could consist of:

- The Headlines (The Story)
- Transmedia Radar Diagram (The Experience)
- Platform Action Chart (The platform traversal/calls-to-action)
- The Reference Guide ("The Bible" - the details)

3.1   THE HEADLINES - YOUR STORY

Not only is it important to be able to pitch your project quickly and simply but I feel that transmedia projects can very quickly become unwieldy and possibly unnecessarily complex. Working on the headlines first puts some boundaries on the project and helps to focus the mind on what you're trying to achieve.

The headlines of your story-experience will include:

- **short synopsis** - what happens in the story? Written in a way that's consistent with the genre.

- **high concept** - how does the story play put across platforms?   The term "high concept" is used a lot in the movie world and I've borrowed it because I think it's a good starting place: It's a paragraph that easily communicates your project .

- **premise** - what are you trying to say? This is the point-of-view of the story

- **theme** - what's the recurrent motif or unifying idea that holds everything together? Try to get this to a single word like "obsession" or "temptation" or "courage"

- **genre** - what audience is going to like this project?

Here's an example for my project Lowlifes:

- Short synopsis

    "Lowlifes tells the fictional story of a drug-addicted San Francisco homicide detective, his ex-wife and the private eye she's hired to spy on him"

- high concept

    "one story told over three platforms – a novella, a web series and a blog. Each platform represents one of three principal characters".

- Premise

    "don't judge a book by its cover"

- Theme

    "home"

Figure 37 High Concept for Lowlifes

3.2 TRANSMEDIA RADAR DIAGRAM - YOUR EXPERIENCE

When reading pitches and proposals at StoryLabs[24], I realized that what I really needed upfront from Producers was a very quick and easy way to see what type of experience I was about to discover. So, from this need to avoid lots of reading, I designed the Transmedia Radar Diagram as shown in Figure 38.

You'll notice that the diagram focuses on the experience and not the technology: there's no mention of platforms or business case or even audience. So there's more that needs to be communicated to get the full picture but this is a great way to get your point across quickly.

There's no absolute scale for the four axes, it's their strength relative to each other. Of course, if you're comparing projects then they need to compare across projects too.

---

24 http://storylabs.us/

Figure 38 Transmedia Radar Diagram

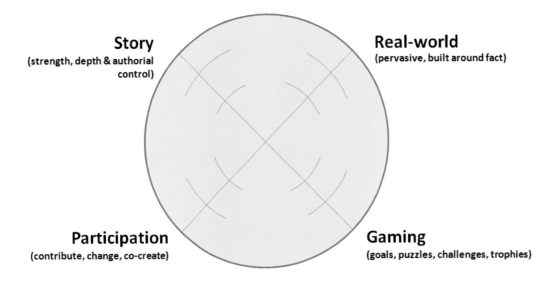

Story = importance of narrative, depth of world & degree of authorial control
Real-world = extent to which story-experience pervades real locations & times, real people & events
Participation = ability of audience to change or contribute to the story-experience
Gaming = audience has goal, use of puzzles, game mechanics (trophies, levels, leader boards etc.)

If you view the original post[25] at Culture Hacker you'll find some example uses of the radar.

3.3 TOWARDS A PLATFORM ACTION CHART

There's an excellent presentation from Christy Dena[26] in which she identifies some key requirements for transmedia documentation:

- indicate which part of the story is told by which media

- indicate the timing of each element

- indicate how the audience traverses the media (what's the call to action?)

- indicate what the audience actually sees and does

- take account of the possibility for "non-linear traversal" through the story

---

[25] http://workbookproject.com/culturehacker/2010/10/12/communicating-your-transmedia-experience/
[26] http://www.babelgum.com/4005320/what-did-they-lessons-learned-crossmedia-christy-dena.html

- provide continuity across developers (who may be working on different media assets)

Christy also references music notation and says that it would be nice to present a transmedia project in this way so that someone could see the beauty of it at a glance.

I've been looking at this approach myself and I'm not the first. I knew that Mike Figgis (who is a composer as well as a director) worked on Timecode[27] using a kind of music notation to present and explain his ideas for four stories would be told simultaneously in real-time. And it's with his kind permission that I'm able to reproduce an example here.   I'd encourage you to check out the movie and the rest of the script.

Figure 39 Mike Figgis' *Timecode*: script page

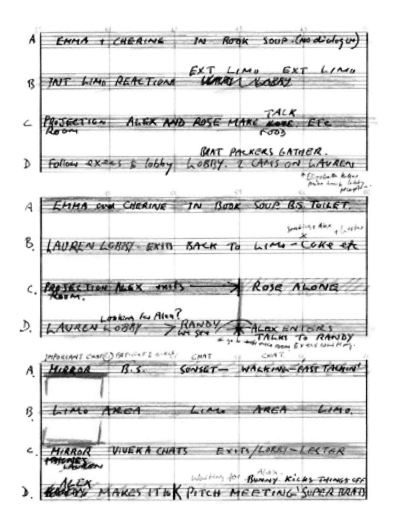

---

[27] http://www.red-mullet.com/home.html

3.4 DISTINGUISHING NARRATIVE FROM EXPERIENCE

In looking at the problems of documenting a transmedia project, my "big idea" was to separate the story from the experience of it. Hence at the highest level we have two timelines: one for story and one for the experience.

Figure 40 Story vs Experience

Greyscale indicates order of release to audience (i.e. order of experience)
Order of release
Available at launch
Possible future/ undefined
Narrative chronology
Story
Chronology of audience experience (eg. story release dates)
Experience

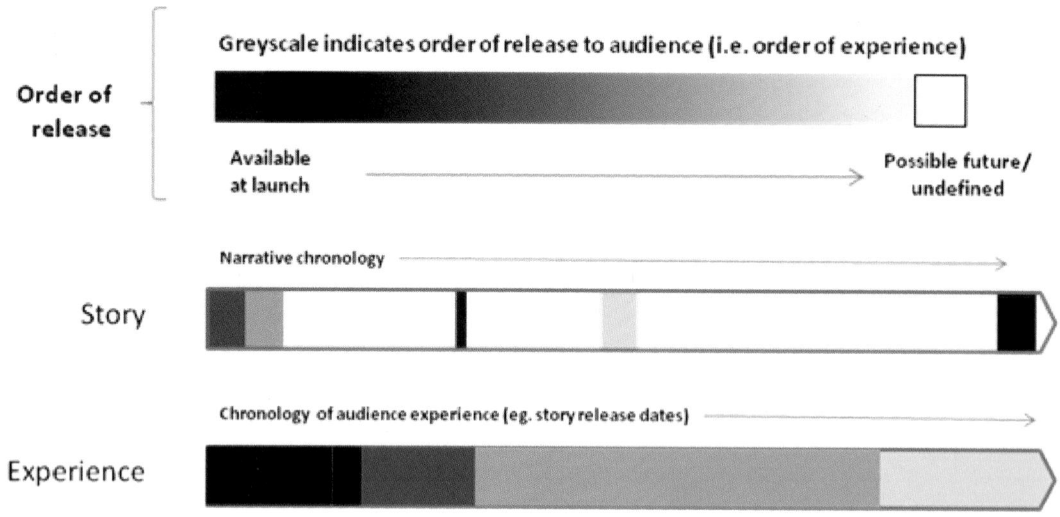

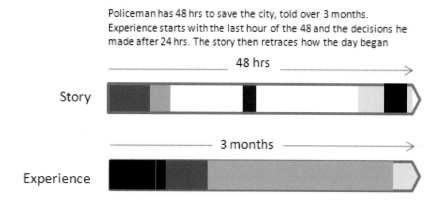

This is best illustrated with an example like the one shown in Figure 2.

Figure 41 Notation Example One

Policeman has 48 hrs to save the city, told over 3 months. Experience starts with the last hour of the 48 and the decisions he made after 24 hrs. The story then retraces how the day began
48 hrs
Story
3 months
Experience
NB: Diagrams show the story intercutting between the end and the middle of the 48hrs with the most audience time given to the final hours before the deadline (which is already known)

Taking this idea further, it's possible to break the media into separate timelines so that it's possible to see which media is being used where.

Figure 42 Story experience by media

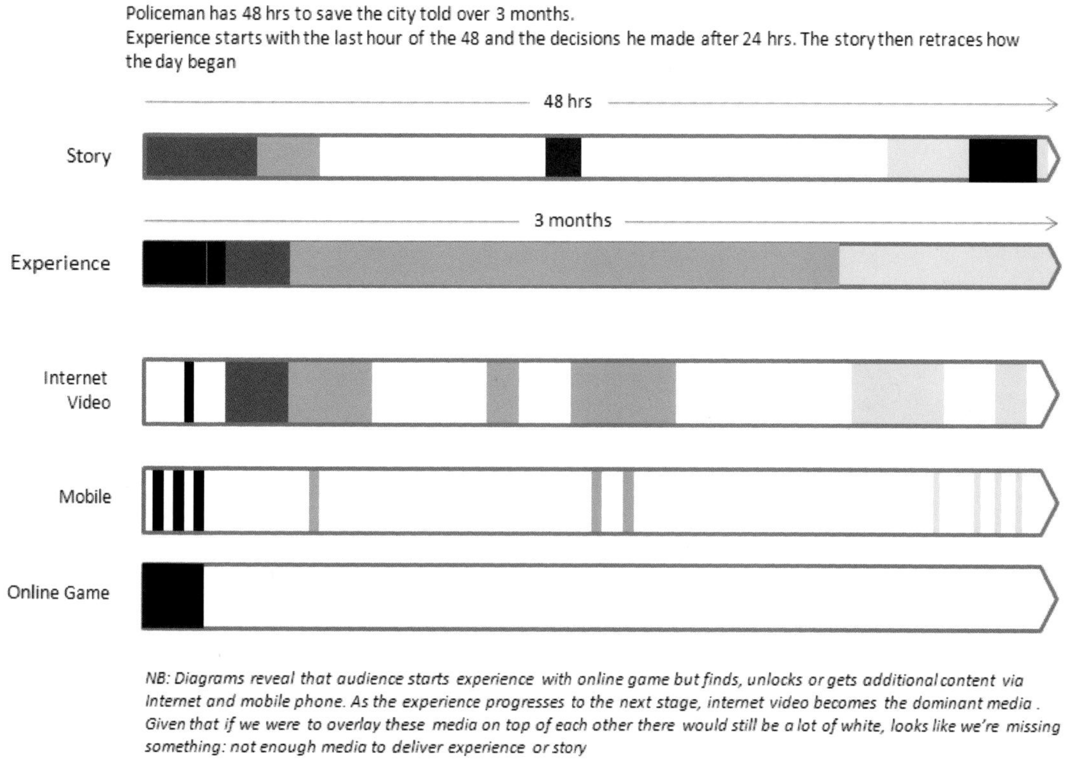
Policeman has 48 hrs to save the city told over 3 months.
Experience starts with the last hour of the 48 and the decisions he made after 24 hrs. The story then retraces how the day began
48 hrs
Story
3 months
Experience
Internet Video
Mobile
Online Game
NB: Diagrams reveal that audience starts experience with online game but finds, unlocks or gets additional content via Internet and mobile phone. As the experience progresses to the next stage, internet video becomes the dominant media. Given that if we were to overlay these media on top of each other there would still be a lot of white, looks like we're missing something: not enough media to deliver experience or story

Hence, at a very high level, it's possible to see in the example above that the audience first encounters the story through an online game which actually reveals the end of the narrative. During the game it looks like there are several mobile media used and some internet video.

At a glance this does meet many of the documentation criteria although it doesn't reveal the detail of how the media is traversed and it's quite time consuming to create.

3.5 TOWARDS A BETTER SOLUTION

To illustrate my improved documentation, I've use the 10 minute ARG created by No Mimes LLC called International Mimes Academy.

The flowchart created my No Mimes LLC is presented in Figure 43. If you're not already familiar with this game, you can download an explanation at the Unfiction forum[28].

Figure 43 International Mime Academy Flowchart

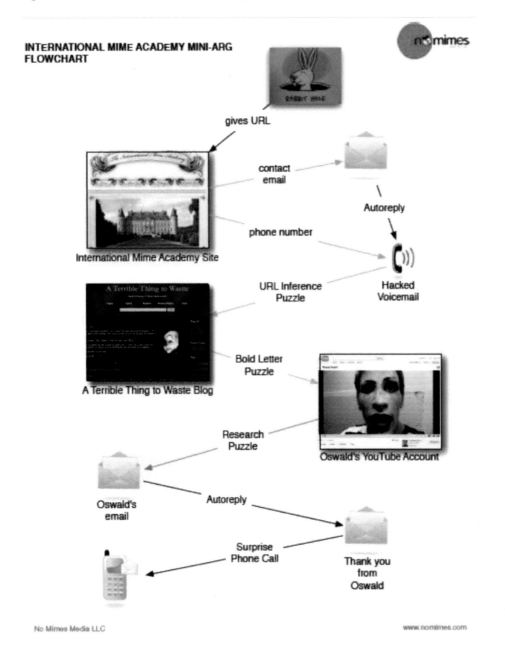

This pictorial flowchart is pretty good because it shows the media and links or calls-to-action between the

_____

[28] http://forums.unfiction.com/forums/files/mime_academy_design_handout.pdf

media and there's an implied sequence of experience (from top to bottom).

Updating my earlier ideas, Figure 44 shows how this flowcart would be represented if the media were separated onto it's only timeline.

Figure 44 Documentation for International Mimes Academy Mini-ARG

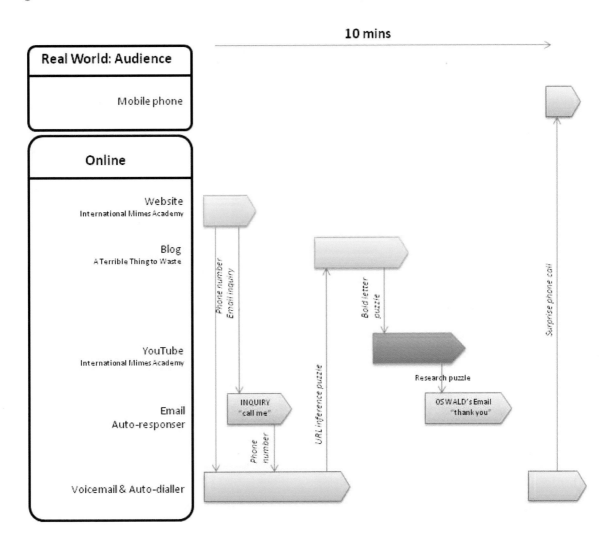

What's good about this approach is that it hits a lot of the goals desired by Christy Dena:

- indicate which part of the story is told by which media

- indicate the timing of each element

- indicate how the audience traverses the media (what's the call to action?)

Separating out the media like this is particularly useful if it's being created by partners or collaborators: it shows what has to be created and how it relates to other media. The colored vectors represent the different platforms and the thin arrows between them document the calls-to-action or bridges between the platforms. I later called this type of chart a Platform Action Chart or "PAC" for short.

The one "exception" that I made for this documentation is the inclusion of the final phone call. Typically I wouldn't' include the audience in the diagram but as it's a concluding part of this experience it felt incomplete without it.

It's difficult to illustrate the strengths of my approach with this simple example. Hence, let's take a more complicated example.

The transmedia project documented in Figure 45 and Figure 46 is called *Colour Bleed* created by Rhys Miles Thomas[29] at Glass Shot in Wales, UK.

Figure 45 Platform Action Chart (PAC) for Colour Bleed: Phase 1 & 2

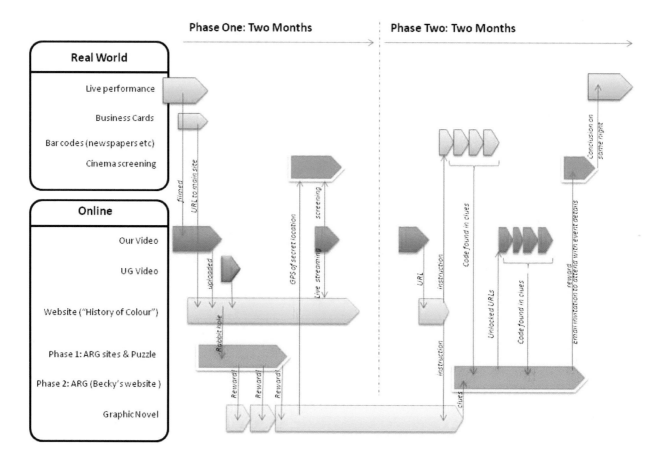

---

[29] http://twitter.com/RhysMT

Figure 46 PAC for Colour Bleed: Phase 3

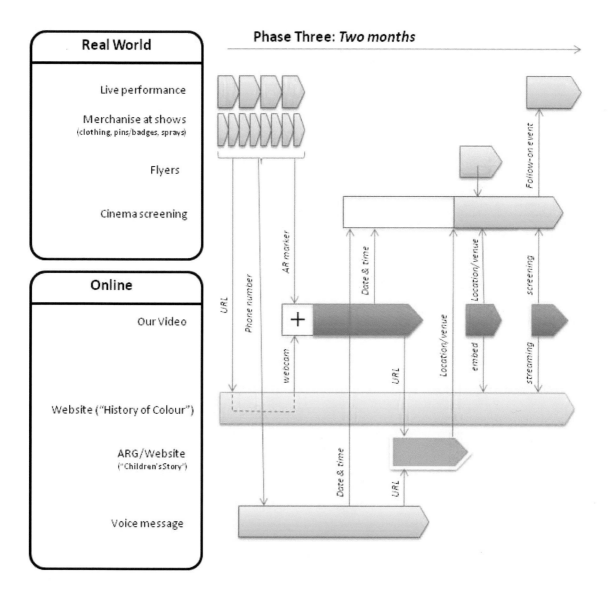

The first thing you see at a glance is the experience runs for six months in three phases each lasting two months and you can see that there are Offline and Online platforms.

You can also quickly see what platforms are being used and their relative timings. So, for example, you can see that "live performance" plays a significant role in this production – starting the experience and ending it. Indeed, *Colour Bleed* kicks-off with impromptu live dance performances at shopping malls and other public place - I've called them "flash dances" ☺ - intended to immediately draw a crowd and attention. But this is the start of a futuristic story in which kids rebel against an authoritarian regime that's banned color and creative expression.

At the flash dances, members of the project team hand out business cards that contain the call-to-action to go online and check out the *History of Colour* website. Note that I've shown two types of video production – "our video", that produced by the project, and "UG video, for user-generated video that we hope will be captured by bystanders on their mobile phones.

Both types of video are hosted at the website and shown as "uploaded". This isn't a call-to-action but it does link and explain how video features in the live performance and on the web. It identifies media that needs to be produced and can be assigned a responsibility.

Other notable things in Phase 1 and Phase 2 are the use of a "rabbit hole" to gain access to the ARG, graphic novels given as rewards for completing phases of the ARG and a series of barcodes given in newspapers to access the second phase of the ARG.

Note that the ARGs are shown as a single platform in this diagram but might they will have their own additional documentation showing a second layer of complexity that's hidden here.

Phase 3 has slightly more complicated documentation because merchandise given away at a series of live events (DJ-led music events and dance offs) offers two paths to revealing the date and time of a final performance:

- A URL to an augmented reality app on the community website that requires the AR marker on the merchandise to unlock

- A phone number to a voice message.

The first video in Phase 3 is shown to require two pieces of information to unlock it – the webcam app and the AR marker on the merchandise.

Note that the final cinema screening is partially colored indicating that although the date & time is revealed, the event can't happen until the location is unlocked.

In some ways one might think that the use of those smaller action arrows are a little inconsistent but I think that's a price worth paying if it helps the objective of creating a simple and effective way of communicating transmedia entertainment experiences.

Finally, Figure 47 shows the quick sketch I did for Heroes of the North[30]. It doesn't look as pretty as the earlier diagrams but it does convey the essentials.

---

[30] http://www.heroesofthenorth.com/

Figure 47 PAC for Heroes of the North ARG (initial sketch)

Narrative Act	WEEK 1 Issue Warnings	WEEK 2 Clues Emerge	WEEK 3 All Seems Lost	WEEK 4 Climax
Game Arc	Establish primary threat: Medusa will release neutron bomb to wipe out all the city's electronics. *They don't say where or when.*	Quests: 1. Find location 2. Find deadline 3. Gather decoder (puzzle pieces) 4. Moral choices?	Clues have all existing clues lead to dead-ends. Heroes are despondent. Thursday: A NEW LEAD! New Hope! Hero's have found some event will happen at start of Week 4 to reveal deadline.	Rapid pace of clues – one per day. The net closes in. More international involvement
Publicity	Get as many local people as possible. Local media & traditional press Flyers, hand-outs etc.			Maximum people anywhere Maximum online & social media activity
Player Success	Needs a handout from the first week of activity – that makes sure it's a local person who gets the prize? ☺		Needs a handout from the first week of activity – that makes sure it's a local person who gets the prize	Special physical puzzle pieces used to defuse the bomb must be collected around town.

ONLINE

Twitter & RSS crisis feeds — VILLAIN sites found?

CDO — Sign-up page: WANTED posters / Community upload area for sightings | HEROES clarify quests in response to VILLAINS | Countdown begins

VILLAINS come out of hidding and reveal their aims (and hence quests)

New Felquists
Medusa

REAL WOLRD

Public Spaces — Go to shopping malls and handout calls for help! Heroes need your support! Have you see this VILLAIN?

Hidden Locations "Drop-boxes" | Digital artifacts: use old tech too like a floppy disc! | Physical pieces left around

Launch Party (LOCATION OF BOMB!)

Week 4 ONLINE column:
Speculation online about what the pieces might be. The handout as a CODE that shows correct ordering of the pieces!
Final tip-off is given at 6am on morning of party
Those arriving at scene must solve the Chinese puzzle with the physical pieces and fit them into the bomb to defuse it!
Have the baddies and Heroes arrive to fight on the scene while the fans try to solve the puzzle!
Have a "fan" as insider filming everything.

3.6 DOCUMENTING THE STORYWORLD

If you're intending for anyone to collaborate on the project – be it the audience, franchisees, subcontractors or whoever – then documenting the storyworld will have a greater significance because it's the primary reference the ensures everyone is "in canon". The word "canon" refers to a set of rules, beliefs, principles, characters, events and so on that are true to the storyworld. Everyone creating content for the storyworld ought to be in canon or else the inconsistencies will create dissatisfaction for audiences because the stories won't ring true. Also, not providing a clear path for collaboration will create problems for you developing your own stories in this world.

Having said this, many fans get satisfaction from creating and consuming fan fiction precisely because it's "out of canon" – it's in a parallel fictional reality to the "authorized" storyworld. Nevertheless one benefit of creating the bible is to distinguish what is part of the world and what is not... although defining what's not part of the world will actually make it part of a larger world... urggh! Enough.

In developing a world you want to create a world that's big enough to give you plenty of scope for multiple stories and characters. Even if you'll only implement a fraction of that world in the first instance, you're laying the ground work for future implementations: series of movies, games, books and so on. I don't believe that a "big enough" world means you need an encyclopedic universe of thousands of characters and locations, I'm saying just don't write yourself into a corner.

The output from this process is often referred to as a "Bible" – it's the holy source that all should refer to and adhere to. The things we might consider documenting would be those shown in Figure 48. Note that in my project workflow this information is shown in the Design stage (see Figure 29).

Figure 48 The Storyworld Bible

1. Storyworld (Mythos)
    a. Timeline – events, wars, treaties
    b. Topography & maps - locations/states/cities
    c. Population
    d. Culture
    e. Religion
    f. Language
    g. Economy
    h. Science & Technology (& Magic)
2. Series synopsis and arcs
3. Future stories

There's a great wiki, an online tool and community for developing storyworlds at ConWorld[31] and I'd also recommend checking out Worldbuilding[32] on Wikipedia.

Note that the bible has only covered the story – not the experience. The experience is documented with the bible in the larger Project Reference Document[33].

---

[31] http://conworld.wikia.com/wiki/Main_Page
[32] http://en.wikipedia.org/wiki/Worldbuilding
[33] http://www.slideshare.net/ZenFilms/transmedia-project-reference-guide-bible

4   PARTICIPATION & ENGAGEMENT

This section provides some advice about how you might determine the content you need and how you might have your audience co-create it with you. There's much that's missing here - particularly in the way of community management - but what there is I think is helpful. I've also included something on viral video which may seem a little out of place but I felt it worth including because it strikes to the heart of what makes content sharable.

4.1   IMMERSION IS NOT ENGAGEMENT

The term "immersion" is often used in transmedia circles to mean that the audience is surrounded by or engrossed in the story. However, I think that immersion is the wrong word to have in mind because it can tend towards clutter - just content (or countless websites) for the sake of having a lot of content and usually dull exposition.

A better mindset is to aim for engagement. Engagement requires each media to be compelling and rewarding. There's a great presentation on SlideShare by Jackie Turnure called *The Rules of Engagement*[34]. Her five point process for audience engagement is:

- Engage – create curiosity and suspense

- Involve – create compelling characters

- Extend – direct audience within and across media

- Surprise – keep audience on the move

- Reward – make it worthwhile.

Experienced cross-platform writer Tim Wright of XPT.com[35] has this bulleted checklist for engagement. He says your story-experience should be:

- Entertaining

---

[34] http://www.slideshare.net/LAMP_AFTRS/rules-of-engagement-jackie-turnure-presentation
[35] http://www.slideshare.net/moongolfer/crossplatform-writing-presentation

- Responsive
- Responsible
- Inclusive
- Playful
- Context sensitive
- Networked
- Social
- Useful

4.2   A CONTENT STRAGEY FOR AUDIENCE ENGAGEMENT

When audiences connect well to your content, they go through three stages of engagement: Discovery, Experience and Exploration as shown in Figure 49.

Figure 49 Three Stages of Audience Engagement

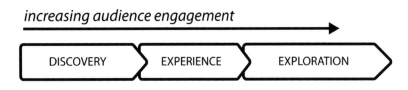

The key to a successful content strategy is understanding (a) that there *are* these stages of engagement (b) what content is required for each stage and (c) what the goals are for each stage.

Failure to appreciate or acknowledge that there are these stages of engagement typically results in audiences being expected to do too much work too soon – which most won't do – and hence the content fails at the Discovery stage and the real experience never begins. Or, expositional-type content that belongs in Exploration is offered as Experience content and hence fails to engage because it doesn't tell a story.

Ignoring these stages is like expecting a kiss from a stranger before flirting with them or expecting to run off and get married after only the first date. Maybe in Vegas, but usually not anywhere else.

With transmedia, one media may act as Discovery content for another.   For example, the comic book serving as Discovery content for a movie or, in the example of the Xbox game *Alan Wake*, six webisodes act as Discovery content for the game.   However, it's important to remember that each media also has its own Discovery>Experience>Exploration stages as shown in Figure 50.

This is particularly important for indies who may think that creating a comic book for their movie will result automatically in an audience for their movie. It won't. The comic book first has to be discovered and experienced and it's only if the content is good enough will the reader begin exploring and "discover" the movie.

Note that I'm fond of encouraging an iterative approach to creating transmedia projects but here I'm also proposing a recursive approach: each and every piece of content should attempt to lure, convince and deliver.

Figure 50 Recursive Nature of Engagement

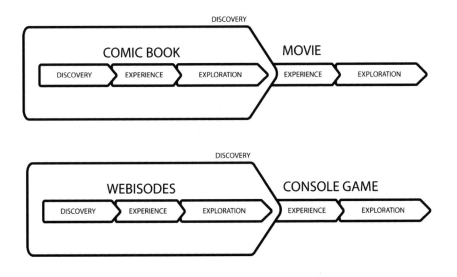

4.2.1 ENGAGING THE FIVE SENSES

Figure 51 uses the metaphor of sensory engagement to illustrate how audiences connect to your content. The concept is that audiences are at first suspicious of new content and that if we are to draw them in and lead them to the highest level of engagement – contributing to the canon – then we must resolves their reservations and satisfy their needs at each stage.

Figure 51 Engaging the Five Senses

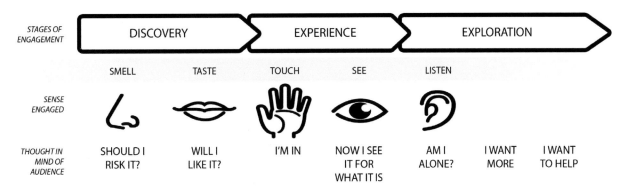

4.2.1.1 *SMELL AND TEASERS*

The first sensory stage is smell. The audience approaches tentatively and sniffs: is there a whiff of the familiar?

We are creatures of habit because evolution has shown it serves us well. Repeating past satisfying experiences is a successful strategy for survival in the wild and with entertainment it's a good indicator too.

The audience needs to be reassured that your content is worth its time and attention. You need to reduce the perceived risk by communicating "trustworthyness", "coolness", "quality", "appropriateness" – whatever values are sought by the audience for this type of project.

To communicate the correct values, I've created a content class called "Teasers". Of course the "teaser" is familiar to indie filmmakers – a 30 second or less video intended to bait the trap; not to explain or reveal too much but only to temp further engagement. In this model however, I've broadened the teaser into a full content category to include all content that can be digested with the minimal amount of attention.

Figure 52 shows the five content classes I've defined for each stage of engagement: Teaser, Trailer, Target, Participation and Collaboration.

Note that I had to create a name for the "target content" to avoid confusion with all the other content! Because of the recursive nature of this approach, any content might be at one time the target content and another time Discovery content.

Note too that because of the need to communicate quickly, visual clues from pictures, photos and web design are going to dominate the Teaser content class. But it's also the headlines you communicate: well-known cast or crew, one-line quotes from reviewers and so on.

Figure 52 Content Classes to Match Stage of Engagement

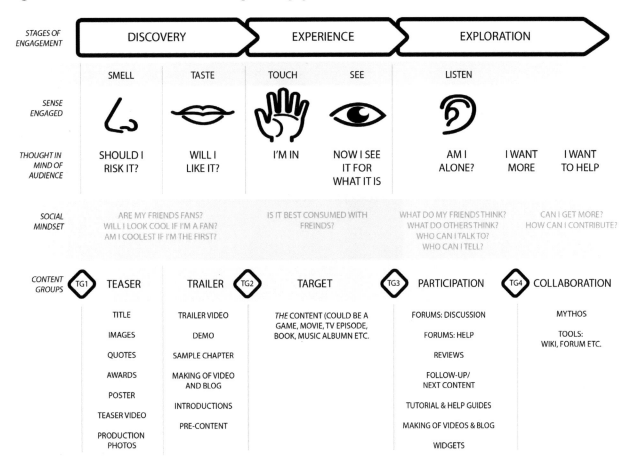

4.2.1.2 TASTE AND TRAILERS

If your project smells familiar then the audience can progress to a more specific, personal question: will I like it?

The teaser has convinced the audience your project is something they *might* like, but what can you tell them to reassure them it's worth their additional time and (possibly) money?

The movie trailer is a commercial. Its intention is to convince the audience that this movie is for them. In this model I've expanded the trailer to a class for all content that persuades. By which I mean content that removes the barrier between Discovery and Experience: it's the barrier between the *known* – the Teaser and Trailer content – and the *unknown* – the target content.

This barrier is represented by toll gate 2 – TG2.

4.2.1.3 TOLLGATES

In this model, tollgates are barriers between one stage and another.

TG1 is tollgate 1. It's the barrier that prevents audiences knowing that your project exists. TG1 can be breached by search engine optimization (SEO), recommendations, links and anything that puts your content on the map. But the first audience encounter should be with your Teaser content.

Tollgate 2 requires a little more explanation.

Think of TG2 as a wall that the audience must climb. Figure 53 shows how the project and business model will unavoidably create barriers to your content – some unintentional, some intentional.

Figure 53 Barriers to Your Content

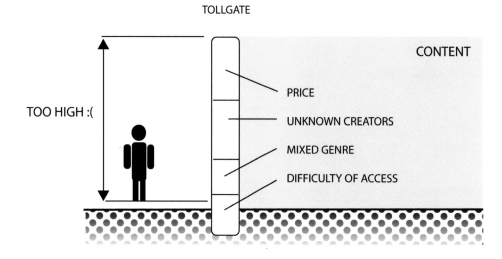

Content that you provide in Discovery helps the audience scale the wall – as shown in Figure 54. In this example, price creates a barrier to entry that of course can only be scaled by the audience paying the fee. However, the tollgate is far higher than solely the price and the audience will only part with its money once the perception of the tollgate is lower than the payment. Stated simply, buyers rarely make decisions not to purchase based on price – it's all those other barriers that have to be overcome first: value, suitability, risk, convenience, context and so on.

Figure 54 Overcoming the Tollgate

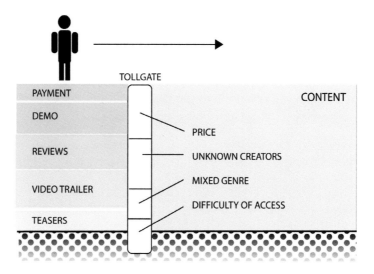

4.2.1.4   TOUCH AND SIGHT

It's only when the audience touches the target content that it can see it for what it is. If your Discovery content has done its job then the audience' expectations will be met or exceeded. But if you have deceived or misled them then they'll be disappointed.

There is nothing more you can do at this point. The target content is what it is. This is what the audience came for and it has to deliver.

After – though sometimes during- the Experience comes the Exploration. The tollgate TG3 is the barrier to be climbed to have the audience increase its *willing* engagement. Sometimes there can be confusion and this will lead to *unwilling* engagement: the audience experiences the content but doesn't quite "get it" and hence searches for an explanation or for help. In these situations of unwilling engagement, a high barrier at TG3 will lead to resentment.

Ordinarily we want the audience to engage further so reducing the height of TG3 should be a priority: make content easy to find and easy to access; signpost what content should follow the target content.

4.2.1.5   LISTENING AND PARTICIPATION

Although content in the participation stage may be available before the Experience, its goal is to aid exploration – not to tease or persuade (even though audiences might use it for reassurance to lower TG2).

Having experienced the target content – either in part or in full – the audience now listens for affirmation. They ask questions to themselves and to others and seek content that answers their questions or fulfils their desire for more.

Good content stimulates debate. Audiences want to discuss and share their experiences with others. They'll also want to extend the experience and will search for add-ons or new target content.

Some audience members will want to show their affiliation to the content by buying merchandise or embedding widgets; they'll want to encourage their friends to try the target content.

Content in this Exploration category is intended to reward and empower the advocate and to educate: it provides additional understanding and value to the target content. In this regard it may be acceptable to have "expositional" content such as character biographies, backstories and so on.

4.2.1.6   COLLABORATION

In this engagement model the ultimate audience engagement is collaboration or contribution. Not everyone in the audience will progress to this stage and some authors may think this undesirable.

Collaboration is not that same as participation. Participation might be passive (reading additional content and exploring the world) or active - voting, sharing, commenting, discussing, Tweeting and so on. Collaboration is adding to the storyworld: writing fan fiction, creating videos or illustrations. It's providing new content that you, as author, are free to embrace or reject.

Between participation and collaboration is tollgate 4 – it's a barrier created by the audience' perceived lack of time and skills, fear of ridicule and lack of information about how to contribute to the world. You can lower this barrier by providing tools, methods, encouragement and a supportive environment.

4.2.2   HOW TO USE THE 5-SENESE ENGAGEMENT MODEL

The premise with this approach is that a transmedia storyworld maybe too vast to expect an audience to jump right in. They have to be teased and led like Hansel and Gretel by a trail of breadcrumbs. Imagine your world to be a huge cavern – if you blindfold your audience and then first open their eyes once they're inside, the vastness is overwhelming – it's a new and scary place. Your audience needs orientation. They have to be guided through an entrance tunnel and see the cavern open up before their eyes and at their own pace. The more complex the world, the more handholding you need to do.

There's also the issue of the time, energy and cost required to digest a whole storyworld. Far better to give the audience smaller snacks at first until their appetite grows for larger, more time-consuming content.

Note that this content strategy is for audience engagement. When combined with the platform selection methodology, start first with revenue-generating target content and see how it might be prioritized by platform. Then use this engagement model to understand the relationship between the platforms and to identify additional content to aid Discovery and Exploration.

4.3   CROWDSOURCING AND COLLABORATION?

Although audience collaboration may not be a prerequisite for a transmedia project, I think we're at the point where the benefits of encouraging collaboration outweigh the problems. The benefits I see relate to the fact that we now work in an overcrowded, competitive and often free content marketplace. Hence, collaboration for me means an opportunity to:

- test ideas and gauge support as early as possible and hence optimize investment of time and money – or give up early

- attract skilled, creative people to ambitious projects too big for either of us to tackle alone

- attract like-minded enthusiasts to help spread awareness in a win-win relationship rather than pestering friends to spam their friends.

So what's the difference between crowdsourcing and collaboration?

Crowdsourcing as implemented in commercial sites like www.99designs.com, www.brickfish.com, www.ideabounty.com or www.filmaka.com tend primarily to be a client pitching a problem in the form of a winner-takes-all competition with the winner receiving a prize, usually a small cash payment. I'd argue that there's not much conversation going on here. Sure, the client asks a question and the crowd shouts back its answers but the crowd doesn't get to influence the requirements or bend the goals towards their needs.

Collaboration to me is more of a free-flowing exchange of ideas wherein the collaborator is able to influence the requirements; which for creative people importantly means a greater opportunity for self-expression. It's the reason why experienced crew might work for less on an independent production: a collaborator feels more like a creative partner than a work-for-hire.

The problem with "collaboration" is that it's more time-consuming to manage and there are issues of maintaining editorial control while still motivating collaborators. It's like directing actors: you have to know what you want without dictating how you get it. Collaboration is not for micro-managers.

But the fact that collaboration is more time-consuming actually works to the advantage of the independent filmmaker who is usually time-rich and cash-poor. Hollywood pays big bucks and they get to decide what happens when and how. Independents should be thinking laterally and using collaboration to leverage what little cash they have rather than struggle to find bigger budgets.

Why Bother?

Here are the reasons I hear most for involving the audience in the creative process:

- the crowd will spread awareness for you by word-of-mouth (i.e. social media) or through the "viral" nature of the task (i.e. getting their friends to vote or comment on uploaded videos, images, mashups etc.)

- the crowd (i.e. many people) will produce better or comparable results for less money

- crowdsourcing is still sexy enough that simply using the approach will generate publicity

- the crowd will produce new insights and being allowed to share their insights will increase their loyalty.

Opinions are divided on whether any or all of this is true; or whether it's ethical; or worth the investment; or worth the risk (perceived or real) of giving the crowd tools to participate only to have them used against you. Plus "professional" creative people argue that amateurs can't be expected to do what they do.

Those for and against can both present evidence in their defense but it seems to me that realizing the potential of crowdsourcing or fan participation is all about framing the participation correctly. And this depends on your objectives and on the crowd: both have to be aligned.

4.3.1.1 RIGHT CROWD, RIGHT GOAL, RIGHT MIND

The diagram below presents a framework for structuring your thoughts about what you might ask the crowd to do, what's in it for them and where you might find them.

Figure 55 Crowdsourcing Matrix

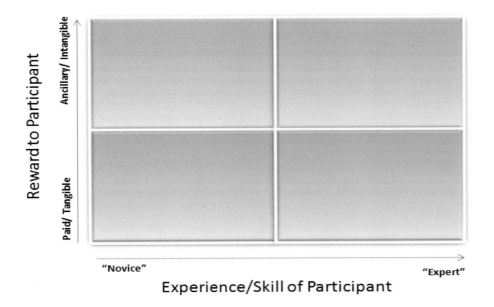

The axes I've chosen are:

- **Experience**. How skilled or knowledgeable does someone have to be to contribute something of value to you?

- **Reward**. What's the incentive or motivation for someone to take part?

If you think of this as "your requirements" vs "their requirements" then success ought to be where the requirements meet.

In the diagram, experience ranges from "novice" to "expert". What exactly constitutes a novice or an expert depends on the task and on your crowd. If you ask an established fan community to tell you which character ought to be killed off then it's probably safe to assume that they'll all be experts. But if you have no fan base to speak of, then even though you're asking the same question you need to assume they're novices.

As a participant, thinking of yourself as a "novice" or an "expert" is important because it determines how you perceive the complexity of the task you're being asked to do. Asking someone with no knowledge of After Effects to blur out a car license plate is a big ask. To someone with even a rudimentary knowledge of AE, it's child's play. Hence it's important to know your crowd.

Here's another example. What if you ask the same fan community to design a new logo for a starship? It's likely that within the crowd there's going to be a spread of abilities and some submissions are sure to be disappointing.   Does it matter that some of the crowd will submit amateurish or poor logos? I guess not if you get one usable logo you like – it only matters if no logos are useable and if you promised to use one of their designs.

With this logo design example, for audience involvement (crowdsourcing) to work you have two options:

- include as part of the prize the prospect of having the fan's logo realized by a professional graphic designer. This would mean that you're more concerned with the process of engagement rather than the actual quality of submissions. It'll make more people feel like experts and hence more are able to contribute

- invite a different crowd – like the one at 99designs – where there's a higher probability of getting a usable design. But don't expect to see significant audience building and retention.

My point here is what's your objective? Is it to get a new logo? Or is it to engage or build a fan base?

4.3.2   DETERMINING THE REWARD

The second axis in the diagram is the reward. You might think that this ranges from "paid" to "unpaid" but that would be a little too simplistic.

Many people take part in crowdsourcing for higher motivational reasons such getting the bragging rights to say they won, getting a kick from others appreciating their work or maybe because they're building a portfolio or a resume. Perhaps it's just the fun of creating or taking part in something. Hence the upper range on the reward axis recognizes that the motivation to participate is more than the prospect of being paid: there are ancillary or intangible benefits to be gained. They might also be incentivized by the prospect of winning a cash prize but the motivation to spend a rainy weekend making a video comes not from the prize itself but from other intangible rewards.

The effect of increasing the cash or making the prize bigger is almost certain to result in more submissions. But increasing the ancillary or intangible rewards will also increase the submissions. If the prize is to have your video shown during the Super Bowl or on Saturday Night Live, then the kudos that bestows is more than having it air on an unknown small business website. Or having a commercial for Sony or Verizon in your portfolio is worth more in terms of enhanced reputation than... a commercial for an unknown small business.

You'll also get more submissions if you're asking the crowd to do less: because now there's a lower bar to clear and more of the crowd will feel capable enough to take part. It makes more of the crowd feel like an expert. But note that what you ask of the crowd is more than just to perform the task itself. It's also how much they are expected to read or agree to before they can contribute and what rights they give up with their submission.

Note too that it's important to balance what you ask of the crowd with the size of the possible reward. Ask too much for too little and not only is it unlikely to produce the desired results but it'll also look like exploitation.

Let's compare two sites that seek to harness the power of the crowd: Brickfish and Filmaka.

- Brickfish[36] asks people with indeterminate skills to do very easy tasks – often as simple as uploading a photo. But they also make the process seem fun and that's because it's the process of engagement with consumers that's important here and not necessarily the end result. I wonder if Brickfish even considers itself to be a crowdsourcing site? Most campaigns are geared more towards empowering advocates or generating views than delivering usable assets.

- Filmaka[37] on the other hand sets the bar much higher. The crowd here is an expert one so it's the end result that's important, not so much the engagement.

4.3.3   STRUCTURING FOR COLLABORATION

Anyone that went to film school is sure to be familiar with those shoots where "collaboration" was taken to mean "everyone tries to do everyone else's job" – which of course results in conflict and disaster. Collaboration ought to mean me doing my job and trusting others to do theirs. But that involves

---

[36] http://www.brickfish.com/
[37] http://www.filmaka.com/

appointing people in clearly defined roles with clearly defined responsibilities. The issue with audience collaboration or open participation is that it can become a free for all. Clearly, to prevent chaos there's a need for collaborators to have some form of guidelines and a structure for how and what they can contribute.

A great insight to these problems can be found in the Purefold presentation by David Bausola, then of Ag8, in which he discusses the aims and needs of the project. David's collaborative transmedia framework has four pillars:

- Editorial: how the story develops with time and with collaboration

- Commercial: presumably how to meet the needs of the brands financing the project

- Technological: how the project is implemented

- Operational: how collaborative input and responses to it are managed. Which for Purefold they hope to be close to real-time.

Another way to break down the problem may be to say that the four cornerstones to be defined for a successful collaborative project are:

- the process, which describes how contributors can participate

- the business model, which describes the financial incentives & rewards, if any, for collaborators

- the legal framework, which describes the contributor's rights and the project's rights

- the platform that supports the above.

One collaborative project worth checking out that has addressed these issues is a multiple media fantasy world called Runes of Gallidon[38]. The project clearly defines and explains:

- the process: contributors (Artisans in their world) must submit work for approval. Submissions are known as "Works" (complete standalone entities, like a short story, say) that contain "Ideas" (elements of the Work, like a character, say, or a location or spell). Only a Work counts towards the revenue share, Ideas are free for all to use

- the business model: if Gallidon makes money it's a 50:50 split for the contributor, if the contributor makes money then Gallidon takes 10%

- the legal framework: Creative Commons +

- the platform: email for submissions, a dedicated site to showcase contributions,   and an online

---

[38] http://runesofgallidon.com/

forum for discussions.

Another example to check out is Wreckamovie.com which has a bespoke platform developed to support its collaborative process. It's cornerstones are as follows:

- the process: project owners pitch tasks; collaborators can "take a shot" which means submit an idea or the piece of work

- the business model: not immediately clear but I think no profit or revenue sharing is assumed

- the legal framework: select one from three Creative Commons licences

- the platform: bespoke collaborative online software that accepts uploads, commenting, notifications and so on.

4.4   WHAT IS A VIRAL VIDEO?

So first, let's define what I mean by a viral video... It ought to be a video that becomes popular because one person recommends it to their friends and they then recommend it to their friends and so on until the video views grow exponentially. So let's say a cool clip that people want to share.

There are those who argue a video is only viral after it's been shared or if it has several hundred thousand views. And Henry Jenkins[39] argues that "viral" is completely the wrong word to use because it fosters the wrong mindset. But "viral video" has stuck with us as jargon and I think it's more helpful to look at "viral video" as a genre - just like music video or short film or feature film.

Note that:

- just uploading a clip to YouTube won't make it "go viral" and those popular clips from well-known brands all have additional marketing support (PR, paid advertising etc) and what's known as "seeding" - outreach to blogs and destination sites asking them to feature the clip.

- although this section exclusively discusses video, the same sentiments can be applied to all social media you'd like to be shared.

4.4.1   SO HOW DO YOU MAKE YOUR VIDEOS SHARABLE?

You have to put yourself in the shoes of the sharer and the receiver. Nobody wants to be associated with lame content, right? So don't create anything that's lame, self-indulgent, pretentious or badly acted unless it's for humorous effect!

---

[39] http://www.henryjenkins.org/2009/02/if_it_doesnt_spread_its_dead_p.html

Ask yourself these questions. When I send someone a link to this video:

- Will I look cool for sharing this video?

- Will it strengthen my friendship with the person I'm sending the video to?

- Will they look cool passing it on?

- Unless you can answer "yes" to all the above then revisit your video idea until you score 3 out of 3.

So here's my advice for optimising your video to make it spreadable:

Spend more time thinking up a great idea than you spend shooting it. This will keep your costs down, keep your enthusiasm high and is most likely to yield the best results.

- Grab attention in the first 5 seconds. Be surprising, be funny, be shocking or tease. Just make sure you grab attention or else you'll be dead in the water.

- Finish with a punch line. There has to be a reward for anyone that's given you up to 30 seconds of their life! Make the last 5 seconds more surprising, funnier, more shocking or more provocative than the first 5 seconds. You want someone to finish the video and think "OMG I have to send this to …."

- Use the middle part of the video to engage. The part between the beginning and the end is the part that needs to keep evolving the idea or revealing something new. If you look at the Levi's viral Guy Backflips into Jeans, it's only about someone jumping into a pair of jeans but the team tries to keep the idea fresh by using different methods and places to jump. It's the same for the Ray-ban Never Hide videos.

Although there's no limit to how long your video can be, it's better to get in, do the job and get out within 30 seconds... 90 seconds tops. Sure, you'll find videos that are longer but you'll find that your time and money is better spent getting those 30 seconds the best they can be than making the video longer.

Invoke a primary emotion in the viewer. Think about which emotion you're trying to invoke in the viewer. Research on viral marketing from the Kelley School of Business at Indiana University found that the best emotions to invoke were surprise & joy. Others possible, although less effective, were sadness, anger, disgust, fear. Although not essential for the viral spread of your video, it's important for the client that the emotions invoked and the connections/connotations brought to mind are consistent with the brand's image and what their fans believe.

Don't make an advert: Your goal is to entertain, not to inform. An advert is different from what I'm defining as a viral video in that it has overt branding, slogans, product details. Virals are much more subtle in their selling - they're entertainment first and a sales pitch a distant second. Creating a great advert is really tough to achieve and if you have limited resources or lack experience then there's a risk that your "viral" will look like a poor advert... which is unlikely to spread. So concentrate on making something entertaining that people want to share.

4.4.2 VIRAL VIDEO STYLES AND FURTHER TIPS

As the world of viral video evolves it's possible to see some similarities among the types of content that's popular online. Note that the styles are not mutually exclusive which means a video's spreadable potential is often helped by combining several styles.

Here are the styles/models I've identified:

- Repeat & innovate: keep it fresh

- Do This at Home/Mash-Up

- How Did They Do That? Did They Really Do That?

- Outrageous (ly Funny)

- Sensational Story

- Surreal

There's also a short discussion here, Cool But Not Viral?, about why these popular videos are not "viral" in the definition I've given above.

4.4.2.1 REPEAT AND INNOVATE: KEEP IT FRESH

Videos that fall into this category are the Levi's Guy Backflips into Jeans and the Ray-ban video Guy Catches Glasses with Face. The Levi's viral is only about someone jumping into a pair of jeans – each jump shown as one shot - but the team tries to keep the idea fresh by using different methods and places to jump and different angles. The idea (of jumping into jeans) is big enough to sustain several iterations. Ditto with Guys Catches Glasses with Face but note how in both the videos the best feat is saved until last – it's the pay-off, the reward for watching until the end.

Both of these videos have the Did They Really Do That? engagement too which prompts viewers to stop, pause and rewind the video – spurring conversation and more sharing.

Thorton's "Stuck" by Harmony Korine is also in this repeat and innovate category but rather than go for amazement and laughs, it's wonderfully touching and by returning to the boy on the bench we get the sense of a story unfolding. The limitation of Stuck is that it creates a warm feeling inside rather than the uplifting rush of success (as with the Levis and Ray-ban videos) and this potentially contributes to less sharing.

4.4.2.2 *DO THIS AT HOME/MASH-UP*

The benefit of a simple idea or a very clear concept is that viewers can spoof it, parody it and mash it up to produce spin-offs that further spread awareness of the original video.

For an example in this category, take Cadbury's Eyebrows. It's impossible to watch and not feel invited to move your eyebrows as the two kids do! Not only does it offer excellent potential to parody with different music and/or different characters but it also invokes the Did They Really Do That question - don't those eyebrows move to fast not to have been enhanced with computer graphics?

4.4.2.3 *HOW DID THEY DO THAT? DID THEY REALLY DO THAT?*

Kobe Jumps Over Speeding Car doesn't have a powerful grab in the first 5 seconds but because it's Kobe Bryant, it's his celebrity and the promise of the video title that gets us hooked. Then he jumps the car and we wonder, did he really do that? Whenever you can provoke a comments war about whether the clip is "fake" or "real" then you've engaged an audience!

I've also included in this style T-mobile's Life's for Sharing although in truth it's a combination of many styles. For example, it's surprising, it follows the Repeat and Innovate model - frequently changing songs and dance moves to keep it fresh, it begs the How Did They Do That? question to stimulate conversation and further enquiry, it even has a just little of the Do This At Home going for it. It's main failing is the weak primary emotion (wonderment) and the lack of a punch line. However, the strength of the Repeat & Innovate and the How Did They Do That? vibes probably overcome the weaknesses but even so, when everyone stops dancing and walks off it's a bit flat after all the energy in the video.

4.4.2.4 *OUTRAGEOUS (LY FUNNY)*

The perfect example of this is the Durex Get It On. This viral scores on so many levels: it's funny because it's taboo (sex, animal sex) yet cute (balloon creatures) so doesn't become gross-out funny and it's technically cool and makes viewers ask "How Did They Do That"?

I've also included in this category a music video for the group Make The Girl Dance. Although not outrageously funny, it's outrageous in the sense of three women walking nude through Paris! The video works not just because of the nudity but because it's excellently executed in one continuous shot (very difficult to achieve), it innovates with different girls, it's humorous & engaging to watch at the bystanders' reactions and it's amazing that they got away with it!

4.4.2.5 *SENSATIONAL STORY*

For this format to work, at its heart there has to be a story that generates conversation around the water cooler - it has to be a sensational story. It's the kind of tale that passes for "news" in the tabloids and gossip magazines - we know it's unimportant but it's fun to talk about. The stories provide light-hearted "humorous shock" and there's often a sense of schadenfreude (which kind of means laughing at someone else's misery).

This is a tough category to get right. A great example is the video below for Triumph Boats. It looks like a candid clip because it's taken in one shot, the picture quality isn't so great and at the end the camera operator runs away leaving the camera running. But it was actually created by an ad agency to highlight & promote the strength of Triumph's boats.

Another, less effective example, is Leaked Assassination Footage from Russia for the video game MIR-12. The problem with this "viral" is that it doesn't invoke any strong primary emotions and it isn't surprising or shocking enough. It succeeds in part because it has a "Did They Really Do That?" interest: it makes the viewer consider if this is actually real footage (although it had us immediately shouting "fake" - the acting & action is too poorly staged and executed to look "realistic"). It's doubtful that this video was actually shared among many friends.

4.4.2.6   SURREAL

This is my last category and ought to be used with caution. It's very easy to say "my video is surreal" when what really ought to be said is that it's confusing! In many ways, most viral videos have some surreal quality to them but it's worth looking at a couple of the best examples.

A classic example of this style is Cadbury's Gorilla. This viral was so ahead of it's time that it generated incredible off-net conversations around the water cooler that further fueled its online growth. More than just surreal though, the video is inventive, engaging, humorous and touching. Investing the gorilla with human traits gives us a warm feeling inside but it also acts as a hook to keep us engaged and in suspense wondering what's going to happen.

Still great but a little less successful is Ray-ban's Cow Gives Birth to Dude. Although it's surreal, it's surprising, it's humorous... it lacks a real feel-good vibe or laugh-out-loud punch line. Massive Yarn Ball Rolls Through San Francisco is better although in a similar vein - it's cool, it's surreal, it's makes you smile but the punch line could just be a little better.

4.4.2.7   COOL BUT NOT VIRAL?

There are many (award-winning) commercials that get shared on the Internet but that doesn't make them a "spreadable". For example, Air New Zealand Nothing to Hide creates a stir because of the nudity/cheekiness and it's certainly inventive but the overt branding and advertising limits it's spreadability - how many more people would have forwarded this video were it not an advert?

The same can be said of Gucci's Flora by Chris Cunningham. Again it's a wonderful video but it's not a viral. Quite apart from the fact that it ends on a pack shot, it doesn't invoke a strong enough primary emotion - joy maybe but it's more of wonderment than happiness.

5   FINANCING

Pulling in an audience is tough and pulling in finance is tougher. This section disucsses:

- the transmedia business model
- audience-pays financing
- sponsored financing:
    - branded entertainment
    - crowdfundng

5.1   THE TRANSMEDIA BUSINESS MODEL

In the "old days" (Figure 56) raising finance was what you did first. You needed that money to make the movie and then you'd sell the movie to a distributor whose job it was to sell it to the audience. Hell, you might even get presales in which case you'd killed two birds with one stone.

The important point from this is that as the filmmaker you only had to convince a limited number of people (investors) that you had a movie worth making (because it would make money). *You didn't have to convince them it was worth watching.*

One reason you didn't have to prove you had an audience waiting to see your movie was because it couldn't be proven. Instead, one might use (often bogus) comparisons with other movies and of course, whenever possible, outliers like *The Blair Witch Project* or *Fahrenheit 911* or *Sideways*.

When the finished movie failed to find an audience it was the distributor's fault. They didn't know how to position the movie correctly. They didn't spend enough money on P&A[40]. The box art was bad.

Figure 56 The Old Model

---

[40] Prints and advertising. This is the money spent getting the movie into cinemas on 35mm film and having an audience show up to watch it.

Having worked with our distributors in some markets and selling directly at some horror conventions, it's very sobering to get a firsthand experience of audience expectations:

> Me: It's about love and sacrifice and how you don't notice you're onto something good until it's gone.

> Horror fan: Great. How much T&A[41] is there?

5.1.1 THE NEW MODEL

When MySpace, Facebook, YouTube etc. arrived it became possible to raise awareness of the movie and start building an audience before the movie was released. But still it felt like something peripheral to the marketing of the movie. The audience building was an industry-side activity that you could take to the distributor with your one-sheet and your reviews: look we have several thousand fans. Most of whom in all likelihood were other independents flogging a movie or a book.

Today, most filmmakers – maybe not readers of this book – but most filmmakers still have the mindset towards social media that it's a new spam tool. Look, now I can pester people to be my "fan" and I can get them to pester their friends to be my "fan". Please Digg me up. Please Stumble on me. It's the worst kind of networking: "please help me" they bleat.

Worst still can be the crowdfunders: "please give me money".   I'm not against audiences paying upfront – as with the Kickstarter model – so it's not the principle, it's typically the execution I have a problem with (which I address in the section on Crowdfunding! Page 93).

And I totally believe in the power of social media but I don't like it when it's so often used in an unproductive, disappointing way.

So enter the new model of filmmaking (Figure 57):

- there's a genuine affection... nay, anticipation... between the audience and the movie

- the affection is leveraged to pre-sell to the audience while still raising finance in the traditional way

- when the movie is available for viewing, it might be that only a subset of the audience will pay for it. So they'll be simultaneous free exhibition and sales.

At this time it's hard to believe that serious money is going to be raised to finance a movie through crowdsourcing. Some money? Maybe. Millions? I doubt it. And so for expensive feature films there's still a place for large-ticket or savvy investors.   Please forget about Obama's fundraising blah blah blah. It's an outlier. And where was his socially networked audience when he needed them to fight for healthcare?

---

[41] nudity

They went missing. Maybe Obama's massive email list isn't really his personal fan base? Maybe the people on that email database were fans of his first movie but don't like his second?

What this says as to us as filmmakers is that we're going to be only as good as our next movie. Don't expect your 1000 mythical spending fans to follow you from movie to movie regardless of what you propose to make.

Figure 57 The New Model

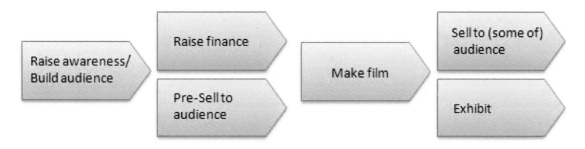

Consequently, approach each project with audience building as early as possible and prove that there's an appetite for what you want to achieve. And so this brings me to my final model.

5.1.2   THE TRANSMEDIA MODEL

Raising awareness and audience building is tough. It's tough enough when you have a finished movie but try doing it for a movie that's yet to be made.

That's why we need a transmedia model for filmmaking in which the filmmaker uses his own money to make some (low-cost) content to build an audience ahead of doing anything else.

There's long been a school of thought that says to get finance for your feature you should shoot the trailer or shoot a short film based on the feature. I know this can work but I've never been a fan of this approach if only because I know finance is most often raised without it. Amazingly though this week (at least when I originally wrote this piece for Culture Hacker), this short film *Panic Attack*[42] secured a movie deal.

What transmedia storytelling offers however is not the Cinderella story of "big investor swoops to finance movie" but a genuine, low-cost, grass-roots audience building.

Right now, (online) comic books seem to be the order of the day – offering an excellent way to engage audiences in the story and show some visual flare or at worst nice eye candy to grab attention[43]. But

---

[42] http://www.youtube.com/watch?v=-dadPWhEhVk
[43] Here's a nice example http://exoriare.com/ and so is this: http://rekill.com/

there's lots of untapped potential for simple social games utilizing Twitter and social networks without the need for coding: we just don't have enough reference cases to illustrate all the possibilities yet. And I'm hoping that our Conducttr[44] platform will unleash a wave of creativity that has hitherto be held back by a cost and technology barrier.

A small word of warning: the content has to have value. It can't be a trailer or marketing fluff – you have to produce the real McCoy if you're going to capture audiences.

In the transmedia business model, the financing, exhibition and fundraising work together in tandem with the potential for the feature film to become self-funding. Remember that it's not all for free. Free is your loss-leader to generate the money. Even if it's "real content" you might still effectively look at it as a marketing cost – it can help to position it in this way to investors. And note that what's free and what's paid will be in flux – maybe changing over time and from media to media.

So in the ideal scenario the filmmaker bootstraps the movie with the low-cost media, the website, presumably some merchandise but then it's up to the audience to decide what happens next.   The filmmaker will use a basket of financing initiatives: free, pre-paid, paid, paid+[45], investment and sponsorship (including brand integration/product placement) to finance the movie.

Figure 58 Transmedia Filmmaking Business Model

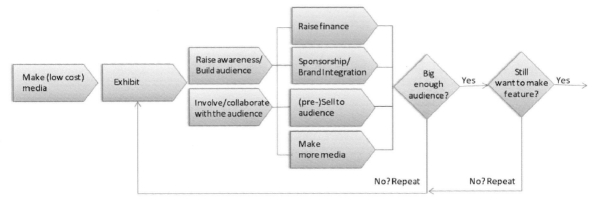

This model has several implications:

- If you do it right they'll be demand for more content... which maybe you can't afford to make in the early days. Or at least can't afford to make alone. And that's why collaboration of all kinds is important to the indie – with audiences and with other filmmakers.   Collaboration platforms like Wreckamovie[46] may save the indie.

---

[44] http://www.transmediastoryteller.com/
[45] Paid+ is where buyers can opt to pay more than the base price – usually via a drop-down menu of price points.
[46] http://www.wreckamovie.com/

- Sponsorship in the form of cash (rather than products for free) from brands won't solely go to properties with big audiences. If your story reaches the audiences that other marketing finds hard to reach then that's going to work too. The one significant problem I can see is that few brands want to be associated with edgy content… unless it's "edgy" in the *Green Day* plastic-punk, manufactured sense rather than the raw, confrontational *Crass/Poison Girls/Flux of Pink Indians* edgy. Counterbalancing this is fans who may appreciate that you've rejected the brands… maybe.

- Filmmakers are going to become familiar with audience needs and they'll learn how to captivate them. It won't be anyone else's fault that you don't have an audience. There's no opportunity to finish the movie and then throw it over the wall to someone else to find the audience for it.

- Free media is a feeler gauge: collect comments, listen to feedback, evolve the feature to meet the audience expectations.

- It's going to be a long commitment to the audience so be sure you pick a story you really want to tell.   Indies that follow this transmedia model will be offering an evolving service rather than a one-off product and that means audiences become customers that need to be listened to, responded to, cared for and managed. This is going to be true for all businesses based on digital content as I explain in the Financing section.

- If you perfect this evolving transmedia ecosystem you may ask yourself if you still want to make a feature after all.

A final sobering thought: I know we'd all like to believe that story is king but audiences will only discover the story if you hook them in. Don't expect anyone to delve deeply into your storyworld looking for brilliance. You have to provide "satellite media" that orbits the core: it's easy to digest and looks cool or fun. Celebrity cast or crew and genre are going to get attention and convey credibility – just as they always have. This teaser and trailer content is discussed in detail in Section 4.2.

I've illustrated this in the figure below where I've taken the sales funnel model and used it to illustrate how you want to pull in audiences, turning casual interest to hardcore repeat purchases.

Figure 59 Matching Content to Audience Commitment

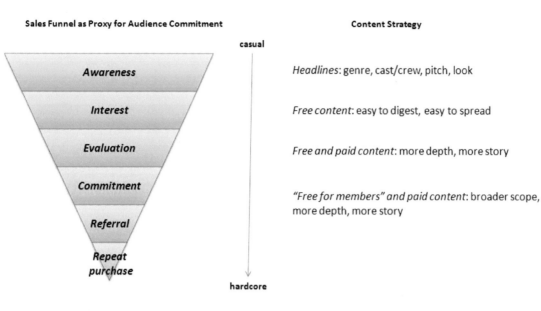

To summarize then, I'm advocating that creative people move to transmedia storytelling because it's going to be the way you build audiences. And building an audience will unlock the financing – either from fans, sponsors or investors.

5.2   AUDIENCE-PAYS FINANCING

With Audience-Pays financing, you're asking the audience to pay for what they consume. Today it feels like an old fashioned idea ☺

The biggest problem with audience-pays financing is that it leaves the creative vulnerable to a market that has increasingly shown itself unwilling to pay (or at least pay to the degree we'd like). I think most would agree that the situation is bad for the traditional model of make-something-and-sell-it-to-everyone-at-the-same-price and it's given rise to a range of pricing models including rental, subscription and pay-what-you-can.

Possibly the most influential ideas to the problem of getting people to part with money when they can often get your content for free are Kevin Kelly's "Better Than Free[47]" and Mike Masnick's now famous equation:

Connect with Fans + Reason to Buy = $$$[48]

---

[47] http://www.kk.org/thetechnium/archives/2008/01/better_than_fre.php
[48] http://www.techdirt.com/articles/20090719/2246525598.shtml

I won't replicate the content of the blog posts I've referenced in the footnotes except to say the main concept is that you must socialize with your audience and sell them something they *value*. The key to success is finding what it is they value and pricing it correctly.

Unlocking the value means understanding your audience and understanding the competition from other products and services. You may feel very strongly that if a video or artwork takes 5 days to complete and you rate your time at $1 per day that you're justified in asking for $5 plus a margin, so say $7. However, if similar products are widely available for $3 (or free) then unfortunately that's the price point in your audience's mind. You must therefore sell something different. It may be that you want to sell essentially the same physical product but you need to find that additional value in the mind of the audience (the consumer) so that they are prepared to pay the $7 you'd like.

In Figure 60 I've worked with the idea that you might sell a "thing" and an "experience" and then looked where the audience might perceive value. So, for example, while some of the audience may not buy a regular DVD perhaps they might if it were personalized in some way. Or, in experience, I'm suggesting that a patron is effectively buying a feel-good experience and not necessarily the product they download or hold in their hands.

A simple example of how your audience might perceive value differently is to look at their balance of leisure time and disposable income: young people will tend to have more leisure time and less money while older audiences may value their time more and hence be more willing to spend money for convenience.

A great resource that discusses the problem of selling content in an era of piracy is Ross Pruden's excellent blog[49] and Twitter panel, #infdist.

Figure 60 Connecting with Fans and Understanding What they Value

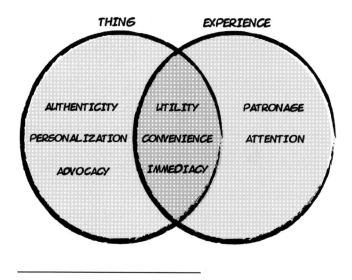

---

[49] http://rosspruden.blogspot.com/

5.3 SPONSORED FINANACING

With Sponsored financing the project is paid for by someone other than the audience consuming the project. I've included in this section:

- product placement and sponsorship

- branded entertainment

- crowdfunding.

5.3.1 WHAT IS A BRAND?

The word "brand" is often used by filmmakers as a short hand for "well-known company". But in marketing terms and the way companies think about "their brand" is much more than that.

To a company, their brand is the sum of all the conversations and opinions that people have about them and their products. "The brand" is the emotional and psychological response from customers when they hear the company's name or see the company's logo or products.

Coke and Pepsi are very similar products but their names illicit very different thoughts, feelings and opinions. That difference is the result of branding. When branding is done well, it's not only what the company says about itself in adverts, it's about how customers are greeted in stores, how the products look and feel, how suppliers are selected and handled.   For example, a coffee shop or supermarket that sells FairTrade products is communicating more about its brand values as any commercial it might produce.

Given the money and time it takes to create a brand – the feelings and associations in our minds when we think of a particular company – you can perhaps appreciate the concerns a brand manager might have with branded entertainment.

5.3.2 PRODUCT PLACEMENT & SPONSORSHIP

Product placement – having a company or product used or featured in your movie – has long been sought after by indie filmmakers hoping to have companies pay towards the cost of production in return for exposure. Newspapers often zing with speculation about how much Nokia, Omega or BMW paid to have their products feature in the latest James Bond movie.

Unfortunately most indie productions are not James Bond. And although your expectations and requests may be modest, the major brands are much more likely to gamble the house on James Bond than flutter a few pennies on an indie production – it's just a safer bet for them.

Fortunately all is not lost if you're flexible with your requests and you think local rather than global.

Public relations is important to most companies as is "corporate and social responsibility" (CSR). You'll find that the big companies in your area support many initiatives aimed at fostering the support of the local community and reinforcing the feeling among employees that this company is a good one to work for. Support under the banner of PR and CSR might be sponsoring local fates and fairs, having a float in the local parade, sponsoring the local soccer team or ballet troupe and it could also be your transmedia project.

And it's not just big businesses - many smaller, local businesses rely on the support and awareness of the local community. Your selling point is not a global YouTube audience - it's the local exposure and local goodwill generated.

For these local companies, product placement maybe not be a requirement at all and a simple "thank you" on the credits or on the publicity materials will do. In fact, you might find that a local company will sponsor a screening, or the publicity for a screening, or give you a product that you can use as a prize to help with driving awareness of your project.

In fact, cash is incredibly hard to get but asking for products and "soft" support is much easier and very often likely to get a "yes". For example, for my movie *London Voodoo* we had the following support:

- Orange UK the mobile company gave us 12 mobile phones with free calling between the mobiles so long as we had a close-up of a phone they were keen to promote

- Subaru gave us two cars to use for the duration of the shoot so long as our hero had one as his family car.

And other productions I've worked on have had free food from fast food outlets.

Although we honored our commitments, nobody from those companies ever came to check and although it wasn't cash support it certainly had a direct impact on our budget.

5.3.3 THE ADVERTISING-FUNDED FEATURE FILM

Figure 61 shows the movie poster for Circumference[50] a film developed by Tim Clague[51] with the intention of being completely advertising funded. Time was quite ahead of his time by a number of years and I recently emailed him to ask what lessons he learned. Here's his answers:

> We had contacts in a few large multi-nationals and obviously started by approaching them. The main issue there was internal politics. Some people would like the idea but others would veto it and basically you couldn't get everyone on the same page at the same time. We were trying to raise £360k at that time - 6 advertisers buying a slot for 60k each. This was a good deal compared

---

[50] http://circumferencemovie.com/
[51] http://projectorfilms.blogspot.com/

with ITV and other ad media at the time. It now isn't as ITV has slashed its rates.

Sometimes companies would say that it seemed too cheap, other times that it was too expensive. It became clear though that without an inside contact there was no way to get into large companies. So we teamed up with social media type ad guys - people who normally sell ad packages for websites etc. That was helpful and I think we had a chance there. Luck was against us with the recession and instant drop off of ad spend.

The concerns all the way through this process were the same however - a lack of history / a lack of a case study. There wasn't really a way around this.

In the current climate I think you would have to shoot it first and try to sell slots later. But even then I'm not sure it would work - a few new different business strategies have come and gone since and times have changed. I think now you would need a successful online series first (eg Mr Vista[52] style) that you then were going to expand.

Epilogue: We have had to ditch this idea of fundraising altogether and are now trying to raise money using the 'old fashioned' methods. I still think, overall, it could work but you would need these ingredients:

1 - already know marketing people high up in big companies and be trusted by them - i.e. be from a marketing / ad producing background

2 - wait until ad rates have risen more

3 - have had a big online success in some form

4 - still be able to shoot cheaply

5 - have a proven niche audience and approach companies who already reach out to that niche.

---

[52] http://mrvista.blogspot.com/

Figure 61 Circumference: An advertising-funded movie

5.3.4 TRANSMEDIA IMPLICATIONS AND IMPLEMENTATION

Turning now to your transmedia project, if you plan to create a comic book or flyer as a give-away or hold an event at a local comic book store to promote your project, you might turn to local companies to:

- provide refreshments for the event (local beer, soft drink and fast food companies)

- pay for the printing (local bookshops, local game stores, local printers)

- provide free publicity (newsletters distributed locally by cinemas, supermarkets and book stores, local newspapers)

Remember that you've created valuable content that audiences want to read or events they want to attend. For some companies, being associated with valuable content and the local publicity produced is desirable.

5.3.5 BRANDED ENTERTAINMENT

Branded entertainment is not product placement or support in-kind. It's about having your content - the characters, the storyline and the production values – embody the brand values.

In fact, product placement – having the product or brand logo frequently appear in shot or appear in a contrived way - can be counterproductive because with this entertainment, reducing the brand presence to a "pack shot" or a blatant promotional message costs the content authenticity and credibility – which of course looses the audience.

In March 2010 I attended the SXSW panel "Web Series 2.0" which included Milo Ventimiglia, Melissa Fallon, Wilson Cleveland, Chris Hanada and journalist Andrew Hampp. Among their credits include the web shows Heroes (Sprint), Rock Band 2 (Cisco), It's a Mall World (American Eagle Outfitters), Gossip Girl: Real NYC Stories Revealed (Dove), The Temp Life (Staples), Easy to Assemble (IKEA).

Much of this section contains a distillation of the wisdom from this panel.

5.3.6   PROMOTING AND DISTRIBUTING A BRANDED WEB SERIES

Distribution is a key consideration for a brand looking at a web series: who will watch it, how many people will watch it and where will they watch it? Producers and brands have to manage the desire for their content to "go viral" with the need to convey the correct brand message.

The goal of the web series depends on the brand and this affects the distribution strategy. For example, to achieve maximum exposure it's best to go where the audiences are and this means syndicating the content as much as possible and making it spreadable. Some brands, however, wanted a series to drive traffic to their own micro-site but this only makes sense if it's an e-commerce site where traffic could be converted to sales.

From my personal perspective, using a series to drive direct sales rather than awareness or promoting a brand message immediately damages the content to the point where it very quickly starts to look like advertising which is hence likely to diminish the desired results.

Audience building should start with those most receptive to your content. Hence with branded content, it's important to get the series in front of the brand enthusiasts. In the case of the series *Easy to Assemble*, the producers approached the top ten IKEA fan blogs. Not only were the blog owners likely to be enthusiastic about the show but they were also gateways to thousands of other fans – hence addressing the distribution problem.

To assist further with distribution, the blog owners were told that whichever blog received the most views would be written into the season finale. This obviously incentivized the blogs to promote the series and drove the total views from all the blogs to 3 million views. The video player given to the blogs to embed on their sites was not spreadable and hence it was easy to track views per site.

Using an actor's likeness and personality to promote a web series certainly helps with distribution but many actors or agents were uncomfortable with branded content if it seems like brand endorsement. This is particularly troublesome when negotiated salaries because brand endorsement attracts a much higher salary than a regular acting fee for appearing in a web series. Hence it's important to stress that the actor is not becoming a spokesperson for the brand, he or she is just helping to promote the shows.

Another consideration when contacting with actors, is if the web series is promoted on TV because this again can cause some friction around salary terms.

5.3.7   OPPORTUNITIES FOR THE INDIE CREATIVE

For the indie creative, working with the biggest brands is going to be tough because of the trouble in reaching out to them in the first place and then being able to deliver on their needs. It's important when pitching to brands that producers have a complete media strategy of which a web series might be one component. Brands want to know how the audience can be retained between webisodes and between web series.

Consequently, rather than approach brands directly, indies might have better luck in approaching smaller advertising agencies and public relations companies who will have a better understanding of their clients' needs and be able to put your content ideas into a wider perspective. Agencies with business-to-business (B2B) clients or clients in unattractive/commodity industries might be most receptive to branded entertainment because of the difficulty in making these companies interesting or remarkable.

Also consider products with niche or difficult to reach audiences. Traditional advertising channels might be prohibitively expensive. For example, *Thread Banger* is a web show aimed at people who like sewing, knitting and making their own clothes. The show, with around 500,000 views per month is perfect for the Japanese sewing machine manufacture Janome. So successful was show sponsorship that Janome now has a sewing machine with Thread Banger branding!

A web show is of course different to a web series – the series is usually fictional and "evergreen" in that it provided entertainment however much time passes since its initial release date. Web shows conversely tend to be more topical, current and factual without a narrative arc. Nevertheless, it does illustrate the opportunity for original content to address a under-served audience.

5.4   CROWDFUNDING

Crowdfunding[53] is a form of Sponsored financing because you're asking people to give you money to fund your project... which you may then choose to give away for free. There's a range of projects and resources at this site: http://crowdfunding.pbworks.com/

If you have a million dollar feature film you'd like to make, I'm skeptical that you can fully finance it with crowdfunding. However, taking the transmedia business model approach, you could successfully use crowdfunding to raise up to $20k to fund part of your project. The right approach though is to consider when, how much and for what to use you'll use other people's money. Asking too soon or for too little will be just as detrimental as asking for too much.

---

[53]   http://en.wikipedia.org/wiki/Crowd_funding

Successfully raising money through Crowdsourcing is all in the planning and your social network. This section presents ideas and information I gained from my work helping people with projects on Kickstarter, from discussions with Andy Baio (Kickstarter's CTO) and Robin Sloan[54]'s panel session at SXSW 2010[55].

A good article you might also check out are these "*10 Tips for Successful Twitter Fundraising*" by Melissa Jun Rowley[56] at Mashable:

1. Cultivate a Strong Community First
2. State Your Purpose and Your Request Clearly
3. Create Buzz and Excitement
4. Have a Strong Set Up Behind the Scenes
5. Have a Powerful Offline Component
6. Plan, Prepare, Execute, then Get Out of the Way
7. Recognize Volunteers and Donors
8. Keep Contributors Up-to-Date on Progress and Needs
9. Keep Track of Developing Relationships
10. Look for Ways to Improve for Next Time

5.4.1 GETTING STARTED

I'm going to assume that you can't keep asking people for money: plan to only have to do it once. That means that you need to think about what you absolutely, can't work around it, specifically and realistically need money for – and then ask once and never again. At least not on this project.

Break down your project into self-contained building blocks. Each block needs a start and end date

Create a masterplan for your project that takes you from the first published content to the finale. Now look at what you can deliver yourself, what you can deliver with collaboration and what you really need financing for. Now you're ready to follow these four stages:

1. Development (pre-campaign)
2. Production (the campaign period)
3. Post-production (after you have the money)
4. Exhibition

5.4.2 DEVELOPMENT (PLANNING)

Make sure what you plan to make is well defined. It must have a start and end date; it must deliver

---

[54] http://robinsloan.com/
[55] http://www.kickstarter.com/projects/robinsloan/robin-writes-a-book-and-you-get-a-copy
[56] http://mashable.com/2010/02/26/twitter-fundraising/

specific desirable content or an experience.

Plan the Production period and determine the best time to launch your crowdfunding campaign. Make sure that you have the resources required to execute the crowdfunding properly: the people, the places, the time, the content. Don't rush out your request for money and then disappear on vacation expecting that the money will be in on your return!

Make sure that someone on the team has a strong following or a good reputation among the desired community. Don't wait to start your fundraising before connecting to audiences because you're creating too big a mountain to climb. Try to make position the crowdfunded content block after you've been able to give something away for free. Use your own resources first before asking others to give you theirs.

Set your reward levels. Take a look at comparable projects on sites like Kickstarter and see how many people are pledging money and at what price-points. At the time of writing, $25 and $50 often look to be the most popular but of course be sure to have some at the $100, $500, $1000 points too - if appropriate.

Write your pitch and make your plea video. Make it personal, passionate, affecting and informative. Tell the story around your story. How will this money change your life or the life of others? How will the money help you realize your ambitions and why should anyone care about that? What will your content mean to audiences or others?

Get your social media in ready. My recommendation is usually that you Tweet progress using your personal Twitter ID rather than create a new one specifically for the project. This way you make a personal connection to people and you can take followers from project to project.

Update your Twitter background to highlight the fundraising campaign, update your Facebook profile photo, update the project Facebook page etc so that all your online presence have calls-to-action directed at your Kickstarter page.

Prepare press releases for the start and end of the campaign. Great journalists want to be the first to learn of great stories. But that means you need a good story and it needs to be newsworthy. Being "newsworthy" means you need to tick some or all of the following boxes:

- Timing – is it happening now or soon?

- Locality – is this appropriate to the readership? If it's a local newspaper then is something happening in town? If it's a site with global readership, is this something of in the right genre and theme?

- Scale & impact – is what you're doing going to affect a lot of people? What's the impact of doing and not doing your project? How important is this campaign?

- Novelty & human interest – if all else fails, will this news make people laugh or cry? Does it have watercoolability?

Make the journalists' job easy and write the article for her. They can always throw yours away and write their own but reduce as much friction as possible – and have nice photos and graphics available too.

5.4.3   PRODUCTION (CAMPAIGN PERIOD)

Design your campaign as you would a story. Plan the campaign period with a beginning, middle and an end. Campaigns typically have lots of activity at the beginning when the call first goes out to find patrons and then at the end when panic sets in! Don't be surprised to find that 50% of your revenue comes in the last 20% of the campaign. Kickstarter knew that having the campaign deadline is a big motivator for getting patrons to commit.

Act 1: Launch the Campaign with a fanfare! Make it exciting and intriguing – make it remarkable so that people want to tell others what you're doing. Consider an offline component that'll generate buzz too – like a launch party. You don't have to hire a private function suite – just find a bar, invite friends and others and bring a soapbox! Wear a T-shirt with a unique Twitter hashtag and encourage everyone to tweet during the evening – create a tweetstorm ☺ And make sure your Kickstarter page is up and running so you can capitalize on the early enthusiasm.

Be quick to respond to questions, comments and patrons.

Act 2: Keep the Dream Alive.

Writing the second act of a script is always the hardest and so it is with the middle of a campaign. You've just hit up everyone you know and you know you'll have to hit them up again at the end. So how do you keep everyone motivated and connected during the middle?

Here's four suggestions:

- Keep the dream alive.
- Give people a reason to retweet.
- Give a mid-campaign sweetner/teaser.
- Combine all of the above.

Keep the Dream Alive.

People want to be on a winning team so frequently update your Kickstarter page with lots of positive energy and upbeat progress reports. We all have those days of anxious self-doubt but don't convey that to the group. You don't have to conceal any problems or disappointments – be open about progress - but greet each hurdle as a challenge rather than an opportunity to moan!

As the donations come in, email each donor to say thank you, ask them if they have any questions and ask for their advice – how can you improve what you're doing? Who else might you ask? Where else might you look for support? People like being asked for their opinion and they like being listen to. Show this love and you'll find that some will take their support to a new level and campaign on your behalf.

For those that donate money above your median price level, ask for their address and send them a handwritten "Thank You" card and maybe a small gift. This isn't something you promised to send, it's a surprise reward for their support.

Give people a reason to retweet

If you're planning a mid-campaign sweetner, that's going to help significantly because, as you'll read next, it's something of value to your community that they'll want to share.

When you reach a certain level of funding – tweet it "25% reached!", "50% reached!"; when that money is enough to buy something important to you – tweet it "Now have enough to buy harddrives! But we still need more to make our target!!!"; when new cast or crew join the team "Rob Pratten is now onboard to direct! But will still need more money – please help"; when a high-spender donates "YES! Thanks to Paul Mackenzie for his AWESOME donation to Project X. But we still need more!"

A mid-campaign sweetner/teaser.

Do something that has value to the audience you're courting. Again it might be an offline meetup or it could be an online live webcast via Ustream or Justin.tv. Give something back and it'll generate buzz, a reason to tweet and cash will come in. Above all – make it valuable and make it interactive.

Act 3: Resolution – the final push. In the closing week, days and hours of your campaign period most people are going to forgive you for making a direct plea for support. In the early stages of the campaign you've been considerate of everyone's time and attention. Now the gloves are off – you have to get that final dollar or you'll lose everything.

Remind everyone how fantastic it's going to be to get the final money and realize your ambition –and keep selling that dream because it's infectious. Think positive but remain focused.

Now is a good time to reach out to bloggers and online news and magazine sites. You can choose to do this at the beginning too but the approaching deadline makes your story more newsworthy because it's more timely.

5.4.4 POST-PRODUCTION (AFTER YOU'VE RAISED YOUR MONEY)

Migrate your patrons from Kickstarter and onto your community page – either Facebook or a forum you've created. Kickstarter is great for fundraising but once the money is in you need to wrap your project around your community and Kickstarter isn't the best place to do that.

Although this is the "post production" phase as far as the fundraising, it's during this period that you'll spend the money creating the content you promised. Keep everyone in the loop and keep them engaged: ask questions, ask for suggestions, show what you've done, report how the money is being spent. Be open and honest.

Your patrons have bet on you and they want reassurance they did the right thing: give it to them - reassure them. Remember too that they're in this for the experience; they're living vicariously though you and receiving enormous pleasure in seeing you succeed. Don't deny them that.

One thing that I have found is that just because someone donates money it does not mean they want to help co-create or get involved in discussions. In several cases I've worked only about 10% of the people who donated money continued to be actively engaged with the production.

5.4.5   EXHIBITION

The big day is finally here! You have something to show that was paid for by many gracious people. Remember why they contributed and allow your patrons to bask in the reflected glory of your success. Your patrons are part of your team and this is another chance for them to feel good about themselves.

The End

I hope you find this document useful and I welcome your comments, insight and feedback. You will find a wealth of examples, tools and people just like you at the Community at TransmediaStoryteller.com

We also offer a free experience design and content management tool called Conducttr that aims to lower the barrier to entry for anyone wishing to tell transmedia stories. Please check it out!

About the Author

Robert is the founder and CEO of TransmediaStoryteller.com an audience engagement company. Robert has a background in telecommunications marketing consultancy (pre-2000) and filmmaking (post-2000) having directed and produced two award-winning, critically acclaimed feature films, London Voodoo and Mindflesh. He is perhaps best known for his advice on transmedia storytelling at Culture Hacker and is the co-host of the Transmedia Talk podcast.

CPSIA information can be obtained
at www.ICGtesting.com
Printed in the USA
LVIC081610270213
321962LV00006B